ULTIMATE GUIDE
PORCHES

ULTIMATE GUIDE

PORCHES

Building techniques for adding a new porch to your home

STEVE CORY

CREATIVE HOMEOWNER®, Upper Saddle River, New Jersey

ULTIMATE GUIDE: PORCHES

AUTHOR	Steve Cory
MANAGING EDITOR	Fran J. Donegan
PHOTO COORDINATOR AND DIGITAL IMAGING SPECIALIST	Mary Dolan
PROOFREADER	Sara M. Markowitz
TECHNICAL EDITOR	Joseph Provey
INDEXER	Erica Caridio, The Last Word
LAYOUT	David Geer, Kathryn Wityk, Glee Barre
FRONT COVER PHOTOGRAPHY	(top) Christopher Nuzzaco/Dreamstime.com (bottom left and middle) Bobby Parks (bottom right) Mark Hryciw/Dreamstime.com
BACK COVER PHOTOGRAPHY	(right and left) Steve Cory (middle) American Deck and Patio

CREATIVE HOMEOWNER

VICE PRESIDENT AND PUBLISHER	Timothy O. Bakke
MANAGING EDITOR	Fran J. Donegan
ART DIRECTOR	David Geer
PRODUCTION COORDINATOR	Sara M. Markowitz

Manufactured in the United States of America

Current Printing (last digit)
10 9 8 7 6 5 4 3 2 1

Ultimate Guide: Porches, First Edition
Library of Congress Control Number: 2009941175
ISBN-10: 1-58011-491-1
ISBN-13: 978-1-58011-491-2

CREATIVE HOMEOWNER®
A Division of Federal Marketing Corp.
24 Park Way
Upper Saddle River, NJ 07458
www.creativehomeowner.com

Safety

Although the methods in this book have been reviewed for safety, it is not possible to overstate the importance of using the safest methods you can. What follows are reminders—some do's and don'ts of work safety—to use along with your common sense.

- Always use caution, care, and good judgment when following the procedures described in this book.
- Always be sure that the electrical setup is safe, that no circuit is overloaded, and that all power tools and outlets are properly grounded. Do not use power tools in wet locations.
- Always read container labels on paints, solvents, and other products; provide ventilation; and observe all other warnings.
- Always read the manufacturer's instructions for using a tool, especially the warnings.
- Use hold-downs and push sticks whenever possible when working on a table saw. Avoid working short pieces if you can.
- Always remove the key from any drill chuck (portable or press) before starting the drill.
- Always pay deliberate attention to how a tool works so that you can avoid being injured.
- Always know the limitations of your tools. Do not try to force them to do what they were not designed to do.
- Always make sure that any adjustment is locked before proceeding. For example, always check the rip fence on a table saw or the bevel adjustment on a portable saw before starting to work.
- Always clamp small pieces to a bench or other work surface when using a power tool.
- Always wear the appropriate rubber gloves or work gloves when handling chemicals, moving or stacking lumber, working with concrete, or doing heavy construction.
- Always wear a disposable face mask when you create dust by sawing or sanding. Use a special filtering respirator when working with toxic substances and solvents.
- Always wear eye protection, especially when using power tools or striking metal on metal or concrete; a chip can fly off, for example, when chiseling concrete.
- Never work while wearing loose clothing, open cuffs, or jewelry; tie back long hair.

- Always be aware that there is seldom enough time for your body's reflexes to save you from injury from a power tool in a dangerous situation; everything happens too fast. Be alert!
- Always keep your hands away from the business ends of blades, cutters, and bits.
- Always hold a circular saw firmly, usually with both hands.
- Always use a drill with an auxiliary handle to control the torque when using large-size bits.
- Always check your local building codes when planning new construction. The codes are intended to protect public safety and should be observed to the letter.
- Never work with power tools when you are tired or when under the influence of alcohol or drugs.
- Never cut tiny pieces of wood or pipe using a power saw. When you need a small piece, saw it from a securely clamped longer piece.
- Never change a saw blade or a drill or router bit unless the power cord is unplugged. Do not depend on the switch being off. You might accidentally hit it.
- Never work in insufficient lighting.
- Never work with dull tools. Have them sharpened, or learn how to sharpen them yourself.
- Never use a power tool on a workpiece—large or small—that is not firmly supported.
- Never saw a workpiece that spans a large distance between horses without close support on each side of the cut; the piece can bend, closing on and jamming the blade, causing saw kickback.
- When sawing, never support a workpiece from underneath with your leg or other part of your body.
- Never carry sharp or pointed tools, such as utility knives, awls, or chisels, in your pocket. If you want to carry any of these tools, use a special-purpose tool belt that has leather pockets and holders.

Contents

PEOPLE ARE DISCOVERING—or rediscovering—the pleasures of the porch. While a deck is fully open to the sky and the yard, a porch has one foot inside and one foot outside, allowing folks to enjoy the wider world from within a cozy shelter. A porch can treat you to a panoramic view of falling rain or even a light snow while you sip a hot cup of tea. Or it is a place where you can relax with a cold drink on a hot day, gently cooled by shade and breezes blowing through.

introduction

PORCH WORDS

DEPENDING ON WHERE YOU LIVE, you may hear some different words used to refer to a porch. People from different areas may disagree on some of the terms. Here are some general definitions:

Conservatory: A glass room, with glass overhead as well as on the sides. It is similar to a greenhouse and often filled with plants; it typically contains furniture for lounging and perhaps dining.

Greenhouse: A room with a glass roof as well as glass walls, dedicated to growing plants.

Portico: A long roofed entryway to a building, often with columns on either side. Porticos are usually found on large official buildings, but a modest portico may serve as an entrance to a colonial-style house.

Stoop: A small stairway leading to a house, especially in urban settings. Typically a stoop has room for no more than a chair or two; visiting and lounging often take place on the stairs themselves.

Sunroom: This may refer to a three-season porch or to an addition with lots of large windows.

Veranda: This old-fashioned term, more common in the South, describes a long, spacious porch with open (unscreened) sides. Verandas often wrap around two or more sides of a house and often have ornate pillars.

Porches are always friendly, but in different ways. A front porch, open to the neighborhood, lets you wave at and chat with passersby on the sidewalk and perhaps invite them in on a moment's notice. A back porch is hidden from neighbors (or at least most of them), making it the perfect place for family and friends to nestle together.

A simple definition: A porch is a deck with a roof. As opposed to a gazebo, a porch is attached to the house. In most cases, it is built of wood and raised at least slightly above ground level, but a porch may also be a masonry patio with a roof overhead.

For a porch to be a porch, it must have a real roof that is attached to the house to keep out rain and snow, not just a pergola or an overhead trellis. A porch's sides may be left open—often the case in dry climates—or they may be screened to keep out bugs. A three-season porch has glass or acrylic panels, perhaps removable or perhaps sliding, to keep the room somewhat warm in early spring and late autumn. However, once you add serious windows and indoor-type heating, then you have an addition—which is beyond the scope of this book.

GUIDE TO SKILL LEVEL

 Easy. Made for beginners.

 Challenging. Can be done by beginners who have the patience and willingness to learn.

 Difficult. Can be handled by most experienced do-it-yourselfers who have mastered basic construction skills. Consider consulting a specialist.

design options 1

WHEN PLANNING A PORCH PROJECT, don't neglect to dream. It costs nothing to imagine possibilities. Even on a budget, you don't have to settle for a cookie-cutter porch. The cost of adding pizzazz or employing shapes and materials that blend admirably with your house's architecture is often minimal compared with the cost of the porch's basic bones.

Whether you'll build the porch yourself, hire a pro to build it, or do some of the work yourself and hire out, say, the roofing and the electrical work, start by gathering ideas. This chapter has photos of beautiful and well-designed porches to help get your creative energies flowing.

WHAT'S YOUR PLEASURE?

All too often, busy people don't want to "waste time" day-dreaming about their ideal porch, and so they dive right into a porch project by drawing up plans and dealing with nitty-gritty things like budgets, materials, and scheduling inspections. However, this get-right-to-it approach can lead to a porch that doesn't quite meet your needs. Take the time to think things all the way through, so you don't end up wishing you had made the porch just 2 feet wider or positioned the door and electrical outlets to better suit your needs.

A SMOKING ROOM

THESE DAYS, when most people cannot abide second-hand smoke, a surprising number of people use a screened porch for a smoking room. Whether you have a cigarette habit, you've learned to enjoy fine cigars, or you indulge in an old-fashioned pipeful now and then, a porch can be just the place. If gentle breezes do not waft the smoke out of the porch, a fan will almost certainly do the trick.

Enormous screened windows, above, make for eye-popping views and effectively blur the indoor-outdoor distinction. They require super-strong screening, available from specialty sources.

An upstairs porch, below, automatically creates a usable space below, making an ideal spot for a patio or deck.

An outdoor fireplace, opposite, makes this screened-in porch an ideal spot to gather with family and friends.

A set of wide French doors opens the porch to the house, making the two spaces nearly one.

Start planning by listing the things you and your family want from a porch. Some possibilities:

▌ A dining area sheltered from the elements but with a distinct outdoorsy feel
▌ A place to read or relax with a drink when the deck or patio is too hot or too cold
▌ A mosquito-free place to toast the setting sun
▌ An inviting entry to your house
▌ A place to get away from the world
▌ A platform from which you can engage your neighbors

▌ A sunny place where you can grow flowers and perhaps place nonhardy potted plants during the winter
▌ An extra room where people can go during parties
▌ An architectural feature that adds visual interest and value to your home
▌ A place for a spa or hot tub

Once you know what you want, you can more easily answer questions about the size, location, and orientation of the porch—as well as amenities such as fans, lights, electrical outlets, and appliances.

A modest front porch has just enough room for a sitting area and a place to stow boots or toys.

WHAT'S YOUR STYLE?

A deck tends to be low, so only its railings tend to visually impact the look of your home. If it looks a bit more rustic than the house it attaches to, the effect will not be jarring; in fact, a change of visual pace can be cute and whimsical. A porch, on the other hand, stands upright, and may account for nearly half of a home's facade on one side. So it's usually best to take a more serious inventory of its details.

Learn something about your home's architectural style so you can make a good match. In most cases, you will want the shape, siding materials, and trim to match the home.

An exception: if your home is very plain and in need of something to relieve the boredom, it may work to build a porch with columns or moldings that add texture.

If you are unsure how the finished product will look, work with a builder or designer who has a computer program that helps you visualize the porch. (See page 62.)

Three similar porches are given individual personalities by differences in color and trim, above.

A starburst gable design and scalloped trim lend personality to a plain design, above right.

"Gingerbread" trim includes turned posts and mini pickets that mimic the railing, middle right.

Slate, brick, and rough wood with little ornamentation make a large TV feel at home, right.

THE TRADITIONAL FRONT PORCH

Many older homes were built with capacious front porches. These usually were not large enough to accommodate a dining table with seats; after all, it would be unseemly to eat a full meal in front of the neighbors! Instead, there was room for a number of chairs, perhaps a swing, and some end tables, so friends could walk up and share a sit, a drink, a snack, and some conversation in shaded comfort. It was a way to be sociable without having to clean the house.

Unfortunately, the advent of mass-produced inexpensive housing, together with a culture where people drove more than walked, spelled the demise of the front porch in many parts of the country. Instead, homes were built with a narrow set of utilitarian stairs just wide enough to get you up and into the house. These minimal porches may or may not be covered, and they often are made of materials—perhaps bare concrete with a tiny railing—that do not complement the house. Many look tacked on, too

small to serve a purpose other than entry into the house.

Adding a real front porch will increase usable space. The roof may provide shade that cuts down on air conditioning expenses in the summer. And if it is well designed, a front porch will enrich the look of your home. A house that is bare and plain in front will be enhanced visually with a porch that incorporates decorative posts, trim along the underside of the roof, and perhaps a railing and skirting below.

Some front porches are wide, perhaps running the full width of the house. But a front porch is usually no more than 6 or 8 feet deep. It may have a separate roof, attached to the house's side, or the house's roof may continue forward to cover the porch. If the porch's floor is more than 2 feet aboveground, there will need to be a railing. Most front porches are open, but if bugs are a concern and you cannot have a screened porch in the back, you may choose to enclose it with screened walls.

Natural brick steps and wood decking provide a warm complement to vinyl siding and trim, left.

Modern composite decking is easy to maintain but looks just fine with older furnishings, above.

Concrete pavers in earthy tones lead to an old-fashioned front porch with fluted columns, opposite.

Design Options

BACK PORCHES

While a front porch announces your presence to the world, a back porch may be completely hidden from passersby. It's a place for settling in with the family, a few friends, or some engrossing reading material. It's also a great place to eat; in fact, many builders report that the major reason people want new back porches is to gain a dining area that has the benefits without the drawbacks of the great outdoors.

Most porches built today are of the backyard variety. More and more people are finding they can enhance the livability of a back deck by enclosing part of it. In most cases, the porch is used for dining, and the deck is used for grilling.

Even though it's in the back, a porch should be designed to match the house's architecture, so it doesn't look like a box that was tacked on to the house. If possible, treat your back porch as though it were in the front and on display to the world; you'll enjoy it and your yard much more that way.

An inexpensive back porch features a shed roof, railings made of treated lumber, and vinyl-clad trim.

HOW MANY SEASONS?

OF COURSE, the length of time that a porch is usable during the year depends on the climate. But in general, a "two-season" porch is either open or screened—meaning that in a cold climate it is comfortable during the last half of spring, the summer, and the first half of autumn. In a hot climate, a two-season porch may be usable during all of spring, only the cooler half of summer, and all of fall.

A "three-season" porch has acrylic or glass panes that are removable or sliding. It can be used all or most of the spring, summer, and fall in cold areas. In warm regions, a fan plus low-e or tinted glass can make it comfortable during all but the hottest days or the hottest times of day.

A "four-season" porch has serious windows and a source of heat and perhaps air conditioning. This comes perilously close to being an addition and will not be a major emphasis in this book.

A high valuted ceiling and floor-to-ceiling screens make this porch a sumptuous place to enjoy the view, left.

A poolside porch is positioned so that bathers can either lounge in the sun or retreat to cool shade, left.

This second-story porch, above, nestles between sections of the house.

COMBOS

Few back porches are the only structure in the yard; most are adjacent to a deck or a patio. This arrangement allows people to choose between a partial outdoor experience and full exposure to the sun and elements—and to step easily and quickly between the two. And most people prefer to cook on a deck or patio rather than in a porch.

For ease of construction, the porch's floor is sometimes

Building an upper deck automatically creates a lower-level porch. A diverter system must be installed so that rainwater runs through decking boards and out to the gutter and downspouts. Several companies make such systems.

on the same level as the deck or patio. However, many people prefer the outside floor to be a step or more down to more clearly define the spaces, and perhaps to make for fewer steps down to the yard. If the deck or patio is below the porch floor, avoid having a set of steps run right up to the door. There should be a landing, at least 3 feet wide, in front of the door at the same level as the porch for easier entry. And doors right at the top of stairs get leaned on and stressed, so they often fail.

Architecturally, the porch can serve as the first step away from the house, making a graceful transition to the less formal deck or patio, which in turn provides a transition to the yard. And you can feel the gradual changes in ambiance as you walk from one to the next.

A gazebo-like porch abuts a similarly shaped deck, so people can easily move from outside to almost-outside.

GRILLING IN A PORCH?

THE IDEA OF FIRING UP a gas or charcoal grill inside the walls of a porch makes people uneasy, and with good reason. Fumes and heat from a grill that is closer than 6 to 8 feet from a dining chair will make for uncomfortable dining. And some fire codes—especially if you live in a condo or other multiunit building—prohibit placing grills near combustible surfaces. Check with your building department or fire department for requirements in your area before holding your first barbecue.

However, if you have a large, open porch with plenty of ventilation, the fumes and heat should dissipate quickly. And if the diners are retreating to the porch to get out of the rain, doesn't the cook deserve the same comfort?

A stairway leads to a narrow deck and the kitchen door, as well as to a bumped-out porch.

SIZES AND USE AREAS

Plan a porch that is large enough to comfortably hold all the porch furniture while people are using it. And there should be room for people to walk around without bumping into things. It's particularly important to have easy access from the grill to the dining area and from the kitchen to the grill and the dining area.

In almost every case, a porch with a real dining table and chairs needs to be at least 15 feet wide and deep. If there will be only chairs and an end table, it can be as narrow as 9 feet.

A simple drawing on graph paper will help you scope out the situation. (See the examples opposite.) Choose your furniture, and measure the amount of space all the pieces will need while being used. For example, a dining chair scoots back 3 feet from the table. Depending on its size and the length of the chains holding it, a porch swing often needs about 7 feet for to-and-fro swinging. In addition, be sure to include 2- to 3-foot-wide traffic paths so that people can comfortably walk past the sitters and loungers and easily get through to the house and to the outside.

An in-porch spa is positioned so soakers can enjoy the views in comfort, above.

A second living room, below, this porch is wide enough for a large conversation area.

PORCH TRAFFIC FLOW

A square rug delineates a snug 7-foot-square area for a dining table with four chairs. This is just enough room, although the person sitting in the corner will have to squeeze in.

Draw your porch and furniture on scaled graph paper to make sure everything will fit.

DOOR LOCATION

ON A BACK PORCH, the door is almost always best situated on a sidewall near the house for two reasons. First, this positioning allows for easy traffic flow from the house to the outside deck or patio and frees up patio space for furniture and living areas. (If the door were at the front of the porch, traffic would need to move through living areas.) Second, a door visually breaks up the lines formed by the porch's posts and screened sections, while a door at the side is much less noticeable.

On a front porch, the situation is different: the stairway is usually positioned so that you walk up the stairs and straight to the entry door with no turns.

OH, THE WIND AND SUN

Spend some time choosing the location and orientation of your porch so that you can take full advantage of the sun when you want warmth and enjoy the shade when you want to cool down. In addition, decide whether you want to maximize or minimize wind.

Let's start with a few facts of the "duh" variety: an open porch allows free movement of air and full sunshine; a screened porch inhibits those elements a bit. Glass or acrylic windows not only keep the room from getting cold but also increase the solar heat when the sun is shining through them.

The combination of roof and trees often means that a few stray beams of light enter a porch, below.

Morning sun is often welcome on an old-fashioned sitting porch, below right.

Things get more complicated when you consider other factors, such as:

▌ the position of the sun at various times of day
▌ the way the sun's arc changes over the course of a year
▌ the many variables of shade trees—conifers provide the same shade year-round, while deciduous trees let in light once their leaves fall—including the fact that trees will grow larger over the years

There are various ways you can control weather effects. You can choose among a number of screening types; some allow more air flow than others, and some provide more shade than others. (See page 82.) If you have glass or acrylic panes, you can also choose tints or low-e filtering to suit your situation. In addition, you may be able to extend an eave out to provide more shade, or you may choose to plant deciduous trees, which provide shade in the summer and less shade in the winter.

Design Options

WHERE WILL THE SUN SHINE?

THE ILLUSTRATIONS below show how the sun moves daily and over the seasons in various parts of the country. During a day, the sun moves from east to west, but its height depends on how far north you are and the time of year. The sun is farthest south on December 21 and farthest north on June 21.

To learn the exact angles of the sun at various times in your locale, visit the U.S. Naval Observatory's Web site, listed in the Resource Guide at the end of this book.

The good news is that a roof will provide more shade in the summer, when the sun is highest, and less in the winter, when the sun is lowest. You may choose to configure your roof and eave to take maximum advantage of this difference.

TRACKING THE SUN

Path of Summer Sun (about June 21)

Path of Winter Sun (about December 21)

N
E
S
W

SUN SPOTS NORTH AND SOUTH

Miami

Minneapolis

December 21: Winter Solstice

Minneapolis

Miami

June 21: Summer Solstice

BLOCKING THE SUN

Porch Roof

Eave

Summer

Winter

Properly positioned eaves can ensure shade in summer and warming sunlight in winter.

A spa should be sheltered from strong winds and kept out of full sunlight during the hottest part of the day. Here, afternoon sun shines on part of the spa, so bathers can choose sun or shade.

Design Options

SIDE PORCHES AND SMALL PORCHES

Even if you don't have room for a porch that can accommodate furniture, consider sprucing up a small set of stairs and a landing with a roof, columns, and perhaps trim detail. Your house will look better, and you won't get wet while fishing out your keys on a rainy day.

In fact, the smaller the porch, the easier it is to afford rich ornamentation and high-end materials. You'll get a lot for your money because a small feature can have a stunning effect.

A back porch with a little extra space can function as a mudroom, keeping dirty boots outside, above.

A porch tucked into the back corner of a house provides a welcoming covered entry.

POSTS AND COLUMNS

A porch needs posts and columns to support the roof. Simple 4x4s or 6x6s will do the job, but posts or columns are usually the most visually on-display elements of a porch, so they should be dressed up to help define the space and blend with the house.

Nowadays it's easier than ever to install or decorate posts and columns. From online sources you can find columns and rich decorative trim made of PVC plastic, polystyrene, and other materials that cut and install easily. Most types can be painted or left white. Check with local building codes to be sure the columns you choose will be strong enough to support the roof.

Another option is to use solid wood posts that have been lathe-turned. These can be stained, painted with solid colors, or painstakingly detailed with sharply contrasting colors to create a "painted lady" look.

A trio of short, sloping columns atop a masonry column lends a playful sense of permanence, left.

Old-fashioned round columns complement a Victorian house with brick steps and a curved facade, above.

RAILINGS, KNEE WALLS, AND SKIRTING

Most local codes require an open porch more than 2 feet above the ground to have a railing. While a deck's railing can be a rustic affair using exposed 2x2s and 2x4s, a porch usually has a more decorative railing. The stairway should have a railing of a matching style. The usual arrangement calls for evenly spaced balusters (pickets) joined to a top and bottom rail. In a modern home, geometric shapes can look great; on a Victorian house, you can go a bit wild with a railing that combines four or five ornamental components.

You can buy premade railing components, often made of PVC plastic or a composite material, or cut them yourself out of wood. Turned wooden balusters are available in a wide variety of styles, and you can have a woodworker make custom-turned balusters to match elements on the rest of the house. A porch railing's top and bottom rails attach to the posts that support the roof. For ease of cleaning and to allow water to run away, there should be a space between the bottom rail and the decking.

A thick top cap and closely-spaced balusters mimic the lines of fluted columns, above left.

Straight lines of 2x2 balusters, above right, create a sturdy classic railing that enhances the home's trim.

Knee walls with contrasting molding, left, have art deco appeal and enclose electrical outlets.

Knotty pine bead-board on the knee wall, opposite, blends with the ceiling for a unified rustic effect.

If a porch is screened in, you could have the screening extend down to the floor, but most people prefer a knee wall to rise 2 or 3 feet above the floor. Three practical reasons for a knee wall: it allows for running electrical cable and installing outlets; it keeps rain and snow out; and it provides a nice ledge for drinks or potted plants. Knee walls are typically framed with 2x4s but can be finished most any way you want. Faux stone facing and wood or composite siding are popular choices.

If the area below the porch floor is exposed, you may choose to cover it up with skirting. Because this area needs to dry out after rainfalls, there should be ample cross-ventilation; lattice is the most common choice. You may want to add an access door so that you can use the area for storage.

SUNROOMS AND CONSERVATORIES

Of course, any porch lets in plenty of sunlight, but a sunroom seeks to up the ray factor with lots of glass. A sunroom allows you to putter with potted plants year-round even in cold climates. Solar heat will supply plenty of warmth, but you may need an auxiliary source of heat for the coldest nights.

Sunrooms make great studios, providing light and natural warmth to inspire artists, architects, and people who like to dabble in crafty projects. If you install tightly sealed windows with double-glazed sashes, a sunroom can be fairly economical to keep warm during winter nights.

A true conservatory has a glass roof, or at least a large skylight or two. Depending on nearby trees, it can provide nearly as much light for plants as an exposed outdoor location, allowing you to grow just about anything. At night, it can be a magical place to recline on a lounge chair and gaze at stars.

It will take careful planning to keep a conservatory comfortable in many parts of the country. During winter months, a conservatory will warm up on a sunny but cold day, even in a cold climate, but at night the room will cool down quickly. On hot days, all that glazing traps the sun's energy, turning the room into an oven; if there are plenty of watered plants, it may be more like a steam room. However, vents, fans, and insulated shades can help keep a conservatory livable much of the time.

A number of online sources provide prefab conservatories and greenhouses. The better ones are not cheap, but they can save plenty in installation costs. These companies also sell greenhouses designed for growing plants—more utilitarian affairs with plenty of glass but not much in the way of architectural features.

The sky's the limit in this conservatory, opposite; the geometric lines of the beams add interest.

Like an oversize bay window, a hexagonal sunroom, above, lets in light from all sides.

The warmth of the winter sun adds a quiet contemplative glow to the greenhouse at right. Shades can be motor or crank operated.

WRAPAROUNDS, VERANDAS, AND PORTICOS

Most new porches are simple rectangles, partly because construction is less expensive that way and partly because a simple shape is easier to blend architecturally with the house. And curves are difficult and expensive to incorporate into a porch. But if you would like to increase living space on two or more sides of your home, consider a wraparound porch.

A wraparound may simply turn a corner, maintaining the same depth on both sides. Or, you can make one side—often on the front of the house—only 6 feet or so deep, while the other side has a depth of 14 or more feet. That way, the front section is a classic sitting area, while the side portion is large enough to accommodate a true dining area. One area may be open, while the other is screened.

The word "veranda" conjures images of gracious summer living—sipping mint juleps on a wicker chair, nodding off while reading the paper, young people sparking on a swinging chair. Veranda living is inspired by a porch that is wide enough to allow for several activities. People generally don't face each other on a veranda, so it doesn't need to be a deep space. Six feet of depth is sufficient for very gentle porch swinging; a deeper porch is needed if rambunctious children want to engage in vigorous to-and-fro action.

A portico is a long entryway. On large buildings it evokes power and officialdom, but on a house it may simply provide a way to get from the driveway to the house without getting wet. A modest portico is an outwardly projecting roof that can turn a small set of stairs into a small porch.

The wraparound veranda above has details that enhance the Victorian charm of the home.

A stately wraparound porch, right, provides shady seating with views in several directions.

A Southwestern-style portico, opposite, features formal columns that seem borrowed from a log cabin.

THE FLOOR

A porch's floor may be rustic decking, or it may be as finished-looking as the interior floors. More often, it is a compromise surface, made of better-than-average decking or interior flooring that is on the casual side.

Choose flooring that will remain durable for decades. On an open porch, you'll need a material that performs as well as outdoor decking. If a porch has screen sections that extend to the floor, exterior decking is also called for. If your design includes a knee wall and acrylic or glass panels that will be used during the winter, then the flooring can be more interior-like.

If you will use strip flooring on a porch that is less than 8 feet deep, it usually looks best to run it parallel with the wall of the house. If the porch is deeper than 8 feet, you may choose to run it perpendicular to the house.

Resilient tiles, made of vinyl or other flexible materials, can be installed on a simple subsurface of pressure-treated plywood. If you want stone or ceramic tile, then the subfloor will need to be very stiff, which can add a good deal to the cost of the project.

(See pages 72–77 for more information on the available flooring options.)

Ironwood decking with spaces between boards is common on a deck but also porch-worthy, above.

Stunning tongue-and-groove ipé flooring is installed at an angle, meeting in a center strip, below.

Slate tiles, opposite bottom, can be installed on a raised deck, but it must be extra strong.

KEEPING OUT THE BUGS

IF A PORCH IS SCREENED to keep out mosquitoes and other pests, the flooring must provide the same protection. Tongue-and-groove and other solid surfaces do this job well. If decking has spaces between the boards, as with the composite decking shown here, then screening must be installed. Screening may be stapled to the tops of joists just prior to installing the decking, or it may be attached to the undersides of the joists.

Composite decking in a beige tone makes a neutral—and easy to maintain—porch floor.

BRICKS, STONES, AND FAUX MASONRY

A porch doesn't have to be a wooden structure—or, at least, it doesn't have to look like a wooden structure. Columns and knee walls can be built with plywood and then clad with faux veneers that convincingly mimic the look of natural stone or brick for a fraction of the materials and labor costs. They can even be installed by a motivated do-it-yourselfer with little or no masonry experience.

A porch may be supported with a genuine masonry wall, as seen on page 52. A wall like this usually needs plenty of ventilation, so the area under the deck can air out. A variety of decorative openings can solve the ventilation problem.

Porches are usually built as wooden decks with walls and a roof. However, a masonry patio can also be covered with a roof and walls. If the patio already exists, you will probably need to cut out portions of it in order to install deep concrete footings to support posts that hold up the heavy roof.

A raised porch usually has a floor made of wood or composite decking, but a variety of systems allows you to install ceramic tile, stone tile, or faux-stone pavers atop wood framing. The resulting floor will be cool to the touch on hot summer days.

The brick walls of a house's exterior make an excellent backdrop for a porch, opposite.

Stucco can be applied over a plywood structure covered with tar paper and wire mesh, above.

Brick walls for a structure like the one above right need to be installed by professional masons.

Masonry bases finished with stucco support graceful tapered columns, right.

CHOOSING A ROOFLINE

When it comes to planning a porch roof, you have three basic options. A gable roof has a ridge perpendicular to the house, with two sloping sides that create a triangle-shaped vertical section in the middle. This is the most common choice because it fits with the look of most houses. However, it often happens that a house window is positioned where you want the peak of the gable roof. This may mean that you will need to build the porch's roof at a lower slope than the roof slopes elsewhere on the house.

A shed roof is a simple flat surface that slopes downward away from the house, making it the easiest and least expensive option. A shed roof lends an informal appearance that may seem out of place on many homes. However, if the house has a modern design or if the roofline will not be highly visible, a shed may be the logical choice.

A partial hip roof has three sloping sides—two on the sides and one in front. There is a shortened ridge, plus two hips—ridges that angle downward from the front of the main ridge. This is the most complicated type of roof to build. It adds visual interest to a house and may best complement a home that has a hip roof or a nearby garage with a hip roof. The slope should match that of the house roof.

A partial hip roof, above right, has a slope that contrasts with the front gables.

While technically not a roof, the floor of this second-level deck creates a sheltered porchlike spot below—a common situation.

A gable roof presents a facade that points optimistically upward.

CEILING FINISHES

A porch's ceiling may recede visually, or it can be covered with finished materials that make it a focal point of interest. As you may expect, the more finished options are also the more expensive.

▌ The least expensive option, shown below, has exposed structural rafters. The roof's plywood sheathing is grooved siding panels (most commonly, "T1-11," which has evenly spaced grooves.) The grooves are installed facing down so that they become part of the ceiling's appearance. The main drawback is that any cables for lights and fans will be exposed, and only pendant lights can be installed—not recessed fixtures. However, if the rafters are made of high-quality lumber that does not have obvious defects and if the rafters are sanded free of lumber stamps and other stains, the look is pleasingly rustic. In most cases, only one cable—the one leading to the ceiling fan—will be visible. The ceiling may be stained or painted, but many people just leave it unfinished.

▌Many people choose to pay more for a ceiling that is finished, usually with tongue-and-groove bead-board, as seen at bottom. The bead-board attaches to the underside of the rafters. This hides all cables and lets you install recessed canister lights. Bead-board may be run parallel with the walls or in a decorative configuration.

▌A board-and-batten arrangement is typically created by attaching finish-grade plywood to the underside of the rafters and then attaching evenly spaced battens made of 1x2 or 1x4. The plywood may be smooth or grooved as shown directly below. Once painted, the result is reminiscent of an old vacation cottage.

This roof was framed in an unusual way—with all the rafters meeting in a point at the center, opposite. Leaving the rafters exposed creates a stunning ceiling.

Tongue-and-groove bead-board painted in classic ceiling white, above, has a formal interior appeal.

The finished bead-board ceiling, right, neatly accommodates recessed lights and ceiling fans, hiding the cables.

Design Options

SCREEN AND WINDOW OPTIONS

If you live in a dry, virtually bugless climate, you may feel no need to screen-in your porch. But if you live where mosquitoes, flies, blackflies, gnats, or other flying pests roam your airspace, screening is necessary for comfort on a porch. In fact, many people choose to add a porch specifically to keep the bugs out. The right type of screening can provide shade and privacy as well. (See pages 82–83 for more information on types of screening materials.)

In order to make a porch usable for most of the year in cool or cold climes, manufacturers offer a great variety of glass or acrylic panels or sashes. Some of these come very close to being actual sash windows as you would have in the rest of the house, but most emphasize screening over glass or acrylic and do not have the full insulating properties of standard windows.

Here are some of the most common screen and window options used on porches:

- Simple screening is stretched and stapled to the porch's framing, and the staples are then covered with trim. This method is easy and economical, and it provides a clean appearance. Some builders avoid this method because if the screening gets damaged and needs to be replaced, you need to remove trim boards to replace the screening. But newer types of super-strong screening are difficult to damage and usually last for decades—and may never need to be replaced.

- Custom wood screen panels are made to fit tightly between the porch's posts, where they may be attached with hardware such as eyes and hooks. At the edges of the panels, the staples are covered with narrow screen molding. The result is a pleasant old-fashioned look with removable panels.

- Manufacturers make kits with metal or plastic channels that can be quickly custom-fit to openings. These are a bit expensive but easy to install. Some people may not like the look of the channels.

- You can also order units that incorporate both screening and glass or acrylic panels or sashes that can be removed or slid downward. These are the most expensive option, and you may have to wait some weeks for them to arrive. They do offer the most comfort during cold weather (or perhaps when it is very hot, if you add air conditioning).

These rectangular screen sections can be made with screen panels, but screening the upper sections is best done by stapling screening in place.

In winter, glass or acrylic panels, left, can replace screens to let in light and sun and keep out the chill.

Screen sections along the floor, above, take the place of a knee wall.

Dark screening with a tight weave, below, offers both protection from the sun and some privacy.

PORCH AMENITIES

Porches are generally simple spaces where you scatter furniture. But adding a few well-chosen features can make life more livable.

■ A ceiling fan inside a porch feels like a breeze under a shade tree, making a porch livable on a hot, still day. See page 60 to determine how many fans to use, and the size of the fan blades. If the fan has a remote control, you can turn it on, off, up, or down without getting out of your chair. A fan may also have a light.

■ Overhead lights may be modest recessed canisters, which have a low visual profile. Or for a decorative splash, go for decorative pendant lights that hang down like small chandeliers. Consider a combination of several recessed lights, plus one pendant light centered over the dining table.

■ Electrical receptacles (outlets) give you plenty of lighting and appliance options. If you have a knee wall, the outlets can be installed all around the porch; otherwise, you can have them only on the house wall. Install ground-fault circuit interrupter (GFCI) receptacles wherever they may get wet.

Ceiling lights and a fan make this porch a pleasant evening retreat.

- A spa or whirlpool is most often placed outside on the deck or patio, but you may want to consider one in the porch. You won't be able to gaze up at the stars, but you will be able to use it more often.
- Adding heat sources brings a porch close to being an addition, but we'll still allow it. Baseboard heaters, either hot-water or electric, can be controlled by a thermostat; perhaps set to 40 degrees or so to keep plants alive during the coldest days. To take the edge off a nippy evening or morning, a simple space heater placed in the middle of the porch can do the trick; just be sure to follow operating instructions carefully for safety.
- More and more, people are incorporating fireplaces into a porch. This is definitely not a do-it-yourself-friendly project and can be pretty expensive.

An old-fashioned porch swing suspended from ceiling rafters is perfect for a lazy afternoon.

Adding a fireplace to a porch is usually a job for pros.

planning the construction 2

PLANNING A PORCH is a balancing act, and you may find yourself moving back and forth as you try to satisfy both design preferences and practical construction realities. If you are adding a porch to an existing house, there will be a whole set of limitations with which you must deal. You'll need to choose your porch's style, size, position, features, and a number of other practical details. This chapter will help you find the best way to make your dreams a reality.

A PORCH THAT WILL LAST

Over the years, builders and inspectors have developed strategies to ensure that a porch will remain stable and firm for many decades. Local building codes have specific requirements and rules designed to ensure four things:

- The foundations, posts, and beams are adequately sized so that the front of the porch and its roof will not sink.
- Joists and other structural elements are sized and spaced so that none of the porch's parts will sag or fail over time.
- The parts are joined together firmly, using special hardware where necessary, to create a strong "load transfer path" so that the porch will withstand high winds and perhaps even hurricanes.
- Where the porch and its roof attaches to the house, flashings and other materials are installed to keep water from seeping into the house's sheathing and structure where it could create rot and other problems.

The "bones" of a porch—the joists, beams, posts, footings, and flashings—will be mostly hidden from view once the porch is completed, but a local inspector will need to see and sign off on them before you install finish materials.

All framing, as well as the foundation, will be inspected before you apply the finish materials. Special hardware, like these hurricane ties at left, hold the framing together during the strongest of winds.

WORKING WITH A BUILDING DEPARTMENT

A PORCH is a major addition to a house, so it is important to get a building permit from your local building department. An inspector will check the work at specifically arranged stages of construction to verify that the structure, the electrical work, and the roofing are up to code.

If you hire a professional porch builder, he should pull the permits and be present for all inspections; he is also responsible for scheduling the inspections—you should not be responsible for this. Be sure the inspector has signed off on the work before you make the final payment to the contractor.

If you will do the work yourself, visit the building department during the planning stage. Find out, first of all, whether you, the homeowner, are allowed to be the contractor. In some areas, you may be required to hire a licensed contractor. You will almost certainly be required to hire an electrical contractor to run cables, connect to the house's service panel, and perhaps install the lights and receptacles as well.

Codes and regulations cover every aspect of construction, including the depth of footings, the spacing and sizes of joists, the type of electrical cable and devices, the roofing, and the attachments to the house. You may have to meet setback requirements as well.

Once your plans have been approved, you'll need to go through three or more inspections. Typically, the footings, framing, electri-

Obtain a building permit, and display it clearly. Put it in a plastic envelope or bag to keep it dry.

cal, and roofing all are inspected at different times.

Treat the inspector with deference, even if you think he's being unreasonable. It's his job to make sure your porch is firm, durable, and dry, and he will probably not accept compromises to standard construction methods. He usually works with building pros and may be less than patient with a do-it-yourselfer. Make it clear that you intend to follow his instructions to the letter. Supply the building department

with all the drawings and materials lists it requires.

Above all, pay attention to the inspection schedule. Don't cover up any work that the inspector needs to see before he signs off on it. Otherwise, he may make you tear out some of your work so that he can see, say, the footings or the framing. Be friendly and courteous with the inspector. Even if you disagree with him, doing it his way will result in a strong porch.

Planning the Construction

UNDERSTANDING PORCH CONSTRUCTION

The illustration below shows the typical parts of a basic porch. Throughout this book you will see many variations on this design, but your porch will likely have most, if not all, of these elements. The descriptions that follow start at the bottom of the structure and work upward. All of the terms will be explained more fully in the following pages.

A *footing*, also called a pier, is a solid piece of poured concrete that supports a post. Local codes determine the size and shape of the footings, as well as how many you must have and whether or not they need to extend below the frost line. A post anchor, partially sunk into the concrete footing, keeps the post in place.

Structural posts, usually made of pressure-treated 4x4s or 6x6s, are vertical members that rise up to support the floor framing. A *girder*, also called a *beam*, is typically made of two or more 2-by boards laminated together and rests on top of the posts. Depending on the length of the porch floor, there may be two or more girders (each of which needs to be supported by footings and posts). The girder supports 2-by *joists*, typically spaced 16 or 12 inches apart. Often, short pieces of bridging, also called blocking, made of the same material as the joists, span from joist to joist in the middle of the run to add strength. At the house, the joists attach to a *ledger*, which is tied to the house itself. The house's siding is sometimes cut out to accommodate the ledger. Flashing is used to waterproof the joint.

A porch's flooring rests on the joists. It may be made of *decking* boards with spaces between, or with tongue-and-groove pieces. *Posts*, studs, or columns rise up from the flooring to support the roof structure. If an open porch is more than 2 feet above the ground, it must have a railing, which usually includes horizontal rails and vertical balusters. If the porch is closed for screening, it may have a knee wall, or the screen panels may go all the way to the floor. Screening panels and perhaps acrylic or glass panels as well fill the spaces between posts, and a door provides access.

Roof framing varies according to the type of roof. A typical gable roof, which is triangular when viewed from the front, has *rafters* that run at a prescribed angle (called the roof pitch). They rest on headers on each side and meet at a *ridge board* at the top. If the

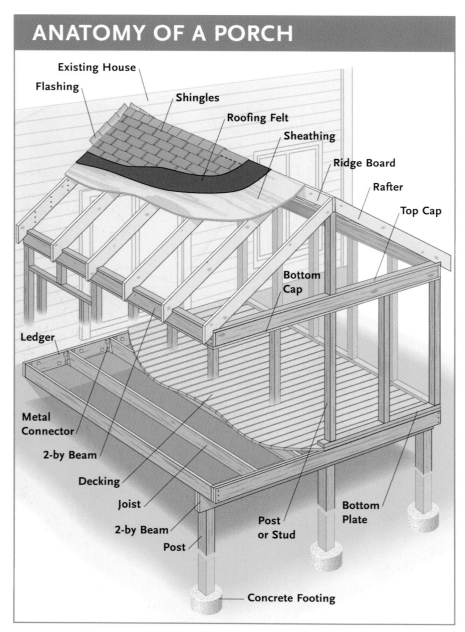

ANATOMY OF A PORCH

Existing House
Flashing
Shingles
Roofing Felt
Sheathing
Ridge Board
Rafter
Top Cap
Bottom Cap
Ledger
Metal Connector
2-by Beam
Decking
Joist
2-by Beam
Post
Post or Stud
Bottom Plate
Concrete Footing

Planning the Construction

ANATOMY OF A SHED ROOF

At its simplest, a porch roof consists of rafters covered by sheathing (usually plywood) and shingles or another roofing material, as shown in the drawing. One end of each rafter is fastened to a ledger affixed to the side of the house. The other end rests on a header supported by the porch posts. The connections of the ledger and shingles to the house are critical for the roof's structural integrity and weatherproofing.

Ledger
Flashing
Shingles
Roofing Felt
Sheathing
House
Rafter
Header
Post
Fascia

ridge is not supported by a post that is in turn supported by a footing, use rafter ties to hold the rafters together. (See page 59.) A shed roof, above, a flat platform that slopes away from the house, rests on a *header* that runs across the front of the porch.

The roof rafters are covered with plywood *sheathing*, which in turn is covered with *roofing felt*, which is topped with *shingles*. Where the roof meets the house, *flashing* keeps the joint dry. Gutters with downspouts run along the sides of a gable roof or along the front of a shed roof.

The basic framing for porch walls is made of 4x4 or 6x6 posts, plus doubled or tripled 2-bys for beams or headers.

Planning the Construction

FOUNDATIONS AND LEDGERS

A porch's foundation must support a seriously heavy roof (not just a pergola), so its foundations must be stronger and more massive than those for a deck. In most cases, a porch's foundation consists of individual footings, also called piers, but if you are planning to build a masonry wall below the porch, it will need a continuous foundation.

FOOTINGS

FOOTING LOCATIONS
Footings should be directly below the posts or columns that support the roof—or no more than a foot away from being directly below.

SIZING AND SPACING FOOTINGS
Local codes determine the diameter and depth of concrete footings. In warm climates, footings need to be massive but do not need to be particularly deep. If you live in an area with freezing winters, the footing must extend below the frost line—the lowest depth to which the ground is expected to freeze. Otherwise, the footing will rise and fall an inch or more during the winter.

WHICH FOOTINGS SUPPORT THE ROOF?
You may be required to make all footings the same size, or you may need to beef up footings that support the roof. A gable roof may have a post that runs up to

the ridge beam that supports the roof, as well as the posts that run up to the headers on the sides. The footings that support those posts may need to be larger than others. On a shed roof, all the footings along the front may need to be larger.

These posts are notched at the top to support a girder.

FOOTING TYPES
The most common footing is a cylindrical column of concrete topped with a post anchor. Other options include a massive footing with a decorative stone or masonry pier on top, or a continuous wall footing topped with concrete blocks.

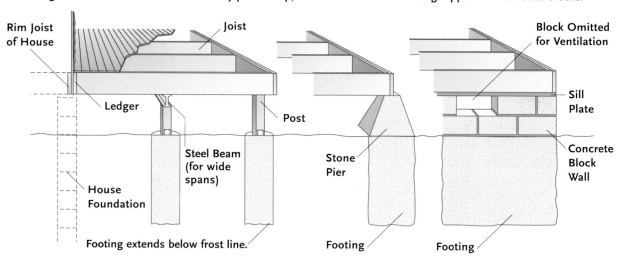

Rim Joist of House
Joist
Block Omitted for Ventilation
Ledger
Post
Sill Plate
Steel Beam (for wide spans)
Stone Pier
Concrete Block Wall
House Foundation
Footing extends below frost line.
Footing
Footing

LEDGERS

ATTACHING TO THE HOUSE WITH A LEDGER

The ledger attachment is critical for two reasons. First, it must be very strong; a number of decks and porches have failed, in some cases leading to loss of life, because the ledger was not attached firmly. Second, it must keep all water out. Inspectors often have specific notions about how a ledger should be attached to the house, and these notions can vary greatly from one area to another.

The most common order of work is to cut out the siding, attach roofing felt or self-stick flashing, install the ledger and joists, add metal or plastic flashing, and finally replace siding down to the flashing. The flashing directs water down and away from the house. However, in very wet areas some builders use a hold-off method: rather than cutting out siding, they attach pieces of composite siding, or other rot-resistant materials to the house, and attach the ledger to the hold-off pieces. Water runs down through the openings.

To attach the ledger, some builders use special "ledger-lock" screws. These are very strong but thin, so they hold firmly and resist breaking yet reduce moisture infiltration around the screw threads. In some areas you are required to bolt the ledger to the rim joist—which means, if the basement is finished, you must cut out a channel in the basement ceiling drywall so you can attach the washer and bolts from the inside.

Ledger-lock screws (inset) are thin but very strong, so they hold firmly and resist shearing, and they limit moisture infiltration better than thicker screws. Here, heavily caulked pieces of composite decking hold the ledger away from the house. Note the caulk on top of the hold-off pieces.

Attach metal flashing after the ledger and joists have been installed. New siding will cover most of the flashing.

BUILDING ONTO A DECK?

IF A PORCH IS BASICALLY A DECK WITH A ROOF, can you simply add a roof to an existing deck? Unfortunately, it's not as easy as it may sound.

- A deck's footings are probably not strong enough to support the roof, so you would need to dig holes and pour new footings—which is difficult to do when the deck is in place.
- A deck's framing often cantilevers out 2 or more feet beyond the footings. Because a porch's posts must be directly above the footings, you may need to pour new footings and install new posts.

- Decking boards are often rustic in appearance and may look out of place in an enclosed porch.
- Because decking boards have spaces between them, they will allow mosquitoes to get in. If the porch is screened, you will need to install netting under the joists to complete the bug barrier.

For these reasons, many builders prefer to demolish an existing deck before building a new porch. However, if you like your decking and the structural issues are not major concerns, it sometimes makes sense to build on top of a deck.

FRAMING AND FLOORING

A porch floor—especially in an enclosed porch—is sort of halfway between a deck surface and an interior floor. It need not look as pristine as an interior floor, but you may not want it to be as rustic as a deck either. And you probably want a floor that is very firm, without the bounciness you feel on many decks.

Framing for the floor is similar to framing for a deck. However, on a porch, joists may be wider and perhaps more closely spaced than on a deck to ensure a rock-solid feel.

All framing is done with pressure-treated lumber to guard against rot. Any piece that comes within a foot of the ground should be rated "ground contact"; other pieces can be rated "aboveground."

Your building department will have span charts indicat-

Some inspectors may require you to install blocking— short pieces of joist material that run between the joists—to add rigidity to the floor framing.

FLOORING OPTIONS

AS IS THE CASE WITH INTERIOR FLOORS, porch floors can be finished with any one of a variety of materials. Because most porches are at least partially exposed to the elements, the finish flooring should be tough and durable.

▌ For many decades, traditional porch flooring was made from **1x4 tongue-and-groove pine or fir,** typically run perpendicular to the house so water would flow away. It must be protected with two or more coats of durable deck paint. This material is still available today, but is not common because it is expensive and not very resistant to rot.

▌ **Ipé and other South American hardwoods** make stunning floors. On a deck, hardwoods need to be stained and finished yearly in most environments. On a porch that is protected from the elements, the floor may need restaining only every few years. Hardwoods most often are in-

stalled as face-nailed deck boards, but some are available as tongue-and-groove boards.

▌ **Cedar and redwood,** often used for decks, are not commonly used on porches. They are available only as decking boards, not as tongue-and-groove flooring. Because they are soft, dents and scratches may occur when furniture is moved across them.

▌ **Pressure-treated decking boards** and tongue-and-groove flooring are the least expensive options. They are often used on informal porch floors, though some people find them too rough looking. Decking boards can be stained to resemble cedar or redwood. Tongue-and-groove treated boards can be painted.

▌ **Composite and vinyl decking** is available as separated decking boards or as tongue-and-groove boards. Most types do not look good as a semi-interior flooring, but some types have variegated colors that ably mimic the look of wood. Many of these products have proprietary fastening systems, including hidden fasteners.

▌ A raised porch floor can be covered with **ceramic or stone tile.** This may be the most expensive option because it starts with a very firm substrate of extra-hefty joists, a plywood subfloor, and concrete backer board or another layer of plywood, which is then covered with tiles that are themselves pretty pricey. However, tile options are bountiful, and the results are beautiful.

ing how far joists and girders can span. The allowable span partly depends on the type of wood you select for the framing and how closely the joists are spaced apart. But be sure to comply with your local codes. Better builders often exceed code, just to make sure their porches are rock solid.

If the porch floor will be open to the elements, it should slope down and away from the house at a rate of 1/4 inch per running foot. That will cause rainwater to flow away from the house.

Tongue-and-groove flooring, a popular choice for porch floors, is blind-nailed, meaning the nails or screws go through the tongues so that their heads are covered by the next piece, as shown on page 96. Standard decking boards are often face-nailed and have gaps between them. Deck boards can also be installed with hidden fasteners, so that the nail or screw heads will not be visible in the finished floor. (See page 78.)

A PATIO PORCH

IF A GROUND-LEVEL PORCH suits your situation, there's no need to excavate to make room for beams and joists. A patio floor can be made of most any masonry material, including pavers set in a gravel-and-sand bed, ceramic tiles set on a concrete slab, or a simple concrete slab with a decorative or stained finish.

To turn a patio into a porch, you need only build a roof over it. In most cases, the patio surface will not be strong enough to support posts that support a roof, so the patio will need to be cut out and footings poured. If you want to screen out the bugs, a pressure-treated sill plate, securely anchored to the patio, should form the base of the framing.

Natural teak tongue-and-groove flooring, lightly stained and sealed, makes for a first-class porch floor.

Tongue-and-grove ipé flooring has a straight grain. Individual boards are usually of one color.

Cumaru has a somewhat reddish tinge, and its grain is more swirly than ipé.

This easy-to-maintain composite decking creates a neutral backdrop for the porch's furniture.

WALLS, COLUMNS, AND RAILINGS

On either an open or a screened porch, walls are kept low to allow an unobstructed view of the yard.

Knee Walls

If the porch will be screened, you may want to install knee walls, which keep floors fairly dry during rains, allow for placement of electrical receptacles, and provide a ledge for placing drinks and potted plants. A knee wall is typically covered with house siding on the outside and beadboard or a board-and-batten combination on the inside.

Columns

Today you can buy expensive-looking columns for reasonable prices. Cylindrical columns made of fiberglass, PVC, and other materials can be purchased from online sources or ordered from a catalog that you find at a home center.

Knee walls, though often low, provide some protection from the elements.

Fiberglass columns, left, are easily installed. Some types are structural, and others are only decorative—meaning you will need to put a wood post inside.

Today, most masonry-look columns, above, are actually made of wooden posts surrounded by a plywood box. Roofing felt and metal lath are applied over the plywood, and lightweight faux stones are mortared on.

Be sure the column will suit your practical needs. Those made of polystyrene, for instance, will not be strong enough to support a roof; you may need to slip them over a wooden post. Some decorative-only columns come in two pieces, so you can easily fasten them around a structural post. Other types are strong enough to be structural.

Masonry columns are typically made by first installing a structural post or posts, then constructing a plywood box. Roofing felt and wire mesh are attached to the plywood, and faux stones are mortared on. The whole process is time consuming, but it does not require special masonry skills. Because the faux stones are not heavy, there are usually no special requirements for enlarging the footings supporting the columns.

Railings

On an open porch, a railing doesn't just provide safety against falling; it also helps to visually frame the porch area. Railings are made of numerous pieces, so it's important to design a railing that securely holds all of the balusters firmly. High-end wooden railings use furniture-like joinery to hold things together. If balusters are simply fastened without joinery, be sure to drive at least two fasteners—screws are usually better than nails—into each joint.

You can buy kit railing systems, often made of PVC plastic, that fit together, so there is very little cutting to do. These are not only easy to install but also strong and reliable. And they come in a good variety of styles that mimic wooden railings.

For a traditional look, use a railing system that consists of turned posts and balusters. Most building codes call for railings for any porch that is more than 2 ft. off of the ground.

ROOF CONSTRUCTION

The roof goes a long way toward defining the look of a porch. Design yours carefully so that it does not look out of place.

Most people prefer the look of a gable roof over a shed roof because it resembles a real house roof. However, in some cases, building a gable roof can be difficult because there is an upper-story window in the way. And building a gable is definitely more work and more expensive than a shed roof. A shed roof takes up less vertical space and is easy to build. And in some cases if the house is fairly modern or more rustic in design, it may be an appealing option.

There are no hard and fast design rules here. When choosing the roof type, do all you can to visualize the finished product—to see how it will look from your yard and from your neighbors' vantage points. A computer design program with 3-D imaging is a great visualization tool. (See page 62.) But you can get much the same effect if you take photos of your house from several vantage spots; then use a felt-tipped marker to draw different roof designs onto the prints.

The most complicated—and most expensive—option is a partial hip roof. It does not rise as high as a gable roof against the house, and so may allow you to build under an upper-story window. It's also a good choice if a nearby roof is of the hip variety.

Roof Slope

A roof's slope is its angle, expressed in two numbers that describe how far it falls every 12 inches. A 3 in 12 (or 3:12) slope, for example, falls only 3 inches per running foot, a very gentle slope, while a 6 in 12 slope is much steeper.

When it comes to roof slope, there are two schools of thought among porch builders. Some firmly believe that a porch's slope should either match the slope of nearby

A porch's roof should complement the rest of the house. Note the short decorative railing on the roof of this porch

house roofs, or at least come very close. Others feel that a porch with a very different slope looks just fine. It is often necessary to flatten a porch roof in order to position its peak under an upper window or other obstruction.

The choice is yours. Take a look at other houses similar in design to yours, to see what appeals to you.

Roofing Materials

Most porches are covered with asphalt or composite shingles that match those on the house. If the house has tiles, slate, or other heavy material, it can be expensive and difficult to match.

If a roof has a slope of 4:12 or steeper, it is usual to cover the plywood with roofing felt (tar paper), then install the shingles. However, if the slope is flatter, you should apply self-sticking ice guard instead of roofing felt to keep windblown rainwater from reaching the sheathing.

RAFTER TIES OR A SUPPORTED RIDGE BEAM

ON A GABLE ROOF, where rafters meet at the peak, downward pressure on the roof causes the rafters to push the walls outward. There are two ways to stop this outward pressure.

First, you could install rafter ties, which span across the room and attach near the bottoms of the rafters. This keeps the rafters from pushing outward and ties the structure together. Some people find rafter ties charming, while others do not like the look of them just above their heads.

As an alternative, support the ridge beam—the board running perpendicular to the rafters at the top of the roof—with a post directly under it in front and a with firm connection to the house at the rear. In this arrangement, the rafters partially hang onto the ridge beam, and do not exert outward pressure on the walls. The advantage of this arrangement is that the roof can have a pristine vaulted appearance. In some cases, horizontal collar ties are installed near the top of the roof to add a bit of visual interest.

Rafter ties can add visual interest while holding the roof framing together.

This low-slope shed roof does not match the slopes on the rest of the house, but it does not feel out of place at the back of the house. When the slope is this low, the roof is considered "flat," and metal or torch-down roofing, rather than shingles, is usually applied.

GUTTERS AND DOWNSPOUTS

PLAN TO INSTALL GUTTERS AND DOWNSPOUTS that match those on the house. In most cases, this means aluminum, but some houses have plastic or even copper gutters. The gutters must be placed at the bottom of a roof slope, but you can sometimes use elbows to move the downspout over to a less visible location. At the bottom of the downspout, you may need to add a drip pad or an extension to direct water away from the house.

Here, drains in the floor of the upper deck direct water into the gutter system, the downspout of which snakes elegantly around moldings near the ground.

ELECTRICAL SERVICES AND CEILING FINISHES

Plan the porch's framing and its finished surfaces with the electrical wiring, receptacles, and fixtures in mind.

Running Cable and Connecting to Power

Many building departments will require you to hire a licensed electrical contractor, at least to make the final connections to the house's power and perhaps to run cable and install all the fixtures and devices as well. In some cases, however, you can do some or even all of the work yourself. Follow the inspector's instructions to the letter because he or she will not tolerate shoddy or incomplete electrical work.

Don't forget the basic rule: never work with live power. Run cable and install fixtures before making the connection to the service panel. Or if the connection has been made, be sure to shut off power to the circuit and then test to make sure power is off before performing any work.

A porch typically has a few 15- or 20-amp receptacles, one or more overhead fans, and some overhead lights. In most cases, you should install a new circuit in the service panel that is dedicated to these services. If you will plug in a heavy electron user, such as an air conditioner or the pump for a spa, that receptacle should probably be on its own dedicated circuit. Check with the electrical inspector to be sure.

If the cable will be covered with finished ceiling and wall materials, most building departments allow you to run standard nonmetallic (NM) cable and install plastic electrical boxes. However, because a porch is a semi-outdoor space, watertight underground feed (UF) cable may be re-

The final connection at the service panel will probably need to be made by a licensed electrician.

SIZING FANS

FAN MANUFACTURERS have charts indicating how large an area various sizes of fan can successfully cool. Usually, you want to buy larger rather than smaller, so you can run the fan on the "low" setting, where it is quietest. In general, a single fan with a 52-inch blade will adequately cool a space from 250 to 400 square feet; use a fan with a 44-inch blade to cool an area from 150 to 250 square feet.

Running cable often calls for drilling strategically placed holes.

quired. In some locales, you must run metal or plastic conduit or metal-clad (MC) cable.

If the wiring will not be covered with finished materials, you may choose to use raceway components. Made of either metal or plastic, these channels and boxes house individual wires or cable. However, raceway may not be allowed in your area, because it is not watertight. On an informal porch, you may run metal conduit, and perhaps paint it. If the porch will be well sheltered from the rain, you may run EMT conduit, but it is usually best to use conduit with watertight connections.

Receptacles and Fixtures

Surprisingly, many overhead lights and fans in porches are the standard indoor variety, with no extra protection against moisture. A little occasional dampness will not harm them. To be safe, however, you may want to install fixtures with watertight housings that are designed for wet areas. Consult with a builder or inspector to determine which types of fixtures to use.

Electrical receptacles (also called outlets) are positioned near the floor and so are more apt to get wet. They should have ground-fault circuit-interrupter (GFCI) protection: either the individual receptacles should be GFCIs, or they should be wired to a GFCI circuit breaker. They should also be housed in watertight electrical boxes, with weatherproof "in-use" covers, as shown below.

WEATHERPROOF BOXES

OUTDOOR EQUIPMENT in constant and unattended use must be connected to a weatherproof box. The cover must protect the box even when the plug is in use.

CEILING AND WALL FINISHES

PORCH CEILINGS and walls are often finished with tongue-and-groove wood bead-board or other decorative wood. Because a porch ceiling stays fairly dry, pine or fir bead-board is often used and is stained rather than painted. Composite and vinyl products that mimic bead-board do not need to be finished.

Covering rafters with boards allows you to install recessed canister lights as well as ceiling fans for a sleek, finished appearance. If you leave the rafters uncovered, you may opt for track lighting instead.

On a timber-type roof, rafters are exposed in an attractive way. In the photo below, 4x6 or larger rafters are spaced 36 inches apart. The roof sheathing is made of 2x6 tongue-and-groove pine, spruce, or cedar. Electrical cable can be run up through the house wall and across the ridge beam; care must be taken to place it where roofing nails will not pierce the cable. In this arrangement, recessed canister lights are not an option, but track lighting is.

Steeply sloping roofs provide a vaulted look. Exposed roof sheathing consisting of individual boards is a popular porch ceiling finish.

MAKING DRAWINGS

Don't neglect to make detailed drawings of your porch project. Not only will the building department want to see where each piece goes; making drawings helps you think through the project and enables you to spot and solve little design problems on paper—which is much easier than fixing them while building. Make three types of drawings: an overhead plan view; two or more side views, also called elevations; and detail drawings of specific aspects of the porch. Also include a detailed materials list.

Producing Scale Drawings

Your building department will want drawings that are to scale. For overall plans, the most common scale is ¼ inch equals 1 foot. This is easy to do using graph paper with ¼-inch grid lines. You may need to buy extra-large sheets of graph paper, or tape pieces together.

These pages show examples of official drawings produced by architects—which is what inspectors most often see. Most inspectors will accept hand-made drawings as long as they give the same sort of information, but your building department may require you to hire an architectural firm to make the drawings. You can make good drawings with basic tools: a pencil, a drafting ruler (which makes it easy to draw parallel lines), and an eraser. You may find it helpful to tape a piece of tracing paper over the drawing so that you can experiment with different ideas.

The Materials List

As you draw, keep a list of all the boards, hardware, concrete, trim, sheathing, roofing, and flashing supplies you will need. This will assure the inspector that you are using the right materials, and it will help you keep track of all the materials you need to buy. Be as specific as possible about the materials. For lumber, indicate not only the sizes but also the treatment ratings, the species, and the grades. (See pages 72–77.) For shingles, indicate the type and their rating in years. Indicate the type of concrete you will use, and give specific manufacturer numbers for the hardware pieces on your porch.

THE PLAN VIEW

THE OVERHEAD PLAN VIEW does not usually include the joists and rafters. It should show the overall dimensions of the porch and the number and positions of the posts. Indicate the sizes and spacing for framing members such as the joists, ledger, rafters, and collar ties. You may also show the locations of fans, lights, switches, and receptacles, or you might have a separate drawing for the electrical service.

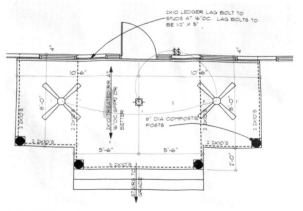

A building department may require a plan view for the porch deck and another for the roof.

COMPUTER DESIGN PROGRAMS

YOU CAN BUY AN INEXPENSIVE CAD program to help you make professional-looking drawings, which you may need when you submit your plans to the building department. These applications make it easy to add windows, doors, lighting fixtures, and the like. Pricier programs allow you to "build" the porch on the screen and then rotate it to look at it from every possible vantage point. You can even add furniture with some applications. If you hire a pro to create a porch design, ask to see your porch plans in 3-D, so you can better visualize how it will actually look once built.

Porch design software will help you produce professional-looking plans. Those with 3-D views allow you to "tour" the porch before building.

ELEVATIONS

MAKE AT LEAST TWO ELEVATION DRAWINGS, viewed from the front and from a side. Draw in many of the framing members, including joists, posts, and rafters. Also include footings and railings. It is common to use a "cutaway" method, in which covering boards and roof sheathing are partially unveiled to reveal underlying framing members. Show enough of the framing members so the remainder can be easily inferred.

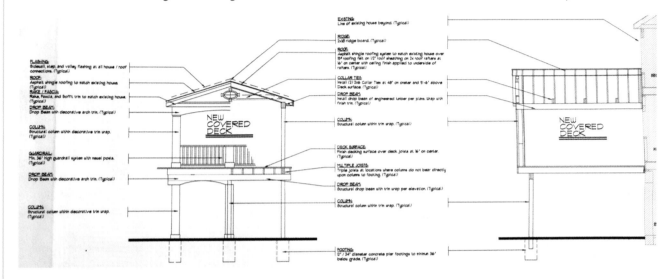

DETAIL DRAWINGS

DRAWING A SMALL PART OF THE PORCH can clearly indicate all of the pieces in ascending order from the footing up to the roofing. A detail drawing can also help you figure out how to make a difficult attachment. In most cases, the inspector will not be interested in the finish trim boards, so you can probably leave most of them out.

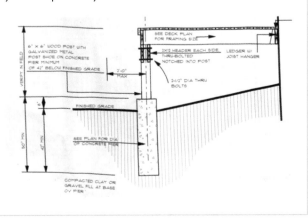

tools & materials 3

A PORCH IS A COMPLEX STRUCTURE. Most consist of a deck—though some are built over a patio—a wall system, and a roof that is complete with gutters and downspots. Most porches have electrical outlets and fixtures, and many have a screening system to keep out the bugs in summer or glass or acrylic panes for cold-weather comfort. This chapter covers the tools you will need to build a porch, and it will help you choose the right materials for your project.

TOOLS

Building a porch calls for plying a variety of trades. Most porches require excavating and pouring concrete; carpentry; roofing; and electrical work. Depending on the design, you may also need to build masonry walls or to clad pillars with faux stones or brick.

Excavation and Concrete Tools

Most excavation can be done with hand tools, though you may choose to use a power auger or hire a company to dig the postholes. Mix concrete in a *wheelbarrow*, which can also be used to transport soil, sod, and gravel. A *posthole digger* enables you to make straight holes by picking up the dirt in bites. You can mix the concrete ingredients together using a *hoe* or a shovel—if you keep it sharp, a *round-pointed shovel* cuts through sod and small roots. *Trowels* smooth concrete. Use a *square-nosed shovel* to dig straight lines in sod. A solid-metal *garden rake* quickly spreads gravel and heavy soil.

Excavation tools. (A) wheelbarrow, (B) posthole digger, (C) standard garden hoe, (D) round-pointed shovel, (E) selection of trowels including a finishing trowel and a pointing trowel, (F) square-nosed shovel with a sharp front edge, and (G) metal garden rake.

Tools for Measuring and Laying Out

Use a variety of tools to ensure that your porch is level, plumb, and straight. A *water level* checks for level over long distances. With a triangular *angle square*, also called by the brand name Speed Square, you can precisely mark for 90- or 45-degree cuts. An accurate 4- or 6-foot *carpenter's level*—aluminum is a good choice—is an absolute must. Periodically check your level for accuracy: set it on a smooth surface, and note the position of the bubble(s). Flip it over end for end and place in the same location; the bubble should be in exactly the same location. A *framing square* quickly checks a corner for square and is used for laying out rafter angles. A *post level* attaches to a post so you can check for plumb in both directions, hands-free. A *folding ruler* measures short distances. A short *torpedo level* is handy for checking short sections for level or plumb. A *combination square* has an adjustable blade that shows 90- and 45-degree angles. A 25- or 30-foot *measuring tape* handles most measuring tasks; for greater distances, consider a 50-foot reel tape. Use nylon *mason's string* to lay out post positions. Use a *chalk-line box* to make perfectly straight lines. To duplicate an odd angle, hold an adjustable *T–bevel* against it and tighten the nut to lock the tool's blade in position. Other useful tools include a *carpenter's pencil*, a *line level* to keep stretched lines straight, and a *plumb bob* to line up postholes with framing.

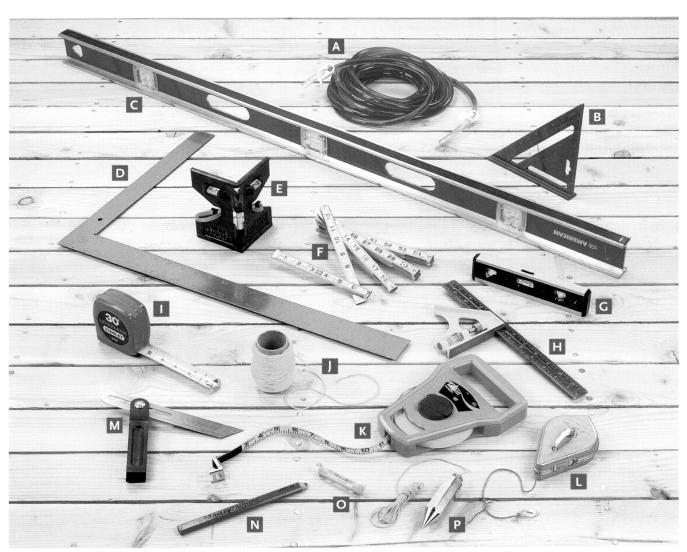

Layout tools. (A) water level, (B) angle square, (C) 4-ft. level, (D) framing square, (E) post level, (F) folding ruler, (G) torpedo level, (H) combination square, (I) measuring tape, (J) string, (K) reel tape, (L) chalk-line box, (M) sliding adjustable T-bevel, (N) pencil, (O) line level, and (P) plumb bob.

Cutting and Shaping Tools

Power miter saw. Also called a chopsaw, a power miter saw is basically a circular saw mounted on a pivot assembly. With it you can make repeatable cuts quickly and with great precision. A 10-inch model will handle most jobs but will not cut completely through a 2x6 at a 45-degree angle; for that you may want to rent or buy a larger saw. If you have a lot of compound miters to cut (in which the board is cut at both an angle and a bevel), you may choose to use a compound-miter model.

Circular saw. You will probably use a circular saw the most of any power tool, so choose one that cuts cleanly and is comfortable to use. A model with a 7¼-inch blade will accomplish most tasks. A quality saw will carry a rating of 12 amps or more. Its base should feel firm and should be easily adjustable for depth and angle. A 24-tooth carbon-tipped blade will cut cleanly and quickly. With practice you can make accurate cuts using a circular saw, but for greater precision use a power miter saw.

Router. You may never need a router for porch building, but the tool makes a rounded or decorative edge on wood trim pieces.

Belt sander. Belt sanders sand quickly, so you need to be careful when using one to avoid gouging the wood. It cannot reach into tight spots.

Reciprocating saw. Use a reciprocating saw for demolition, cutting off posts, and finishing cutouts. Other tools may perform many tasks, but much more slowly.

Saber saw. Also called a jigsaw, a saber saw makes curved cuts and finishes notches cut with a circular saw. Get a heavy-duty model; a cheap one will cut slowly and unsteadily through 2-by lumber.

Pad sander. A vibrating or oscillating sander, the pad sander gets into corners and is usually the best tool for smoothing edges and removing stains or markings.

Block plane. Straightens irregular corners and creates small bevels. Set the blade correctly, and you can use the tool to trim one thin shaving of wood at a time, creating tight-fitting joints.

Other hand tools. A *sanding block* aids in finishing work. Keep a *handsaw* and *hacksaw* on the site for cutting chores. You'll need a sharp *chisel* to clean out notches and dado joints. *Aviation snips*, also called tin snips, cut metal and vinyl flashings.

Cutting and sanding tools.
(A) power miter saw,
(B) circular saw, (C) router,
(D) belt sander, (E) reciprocating saw, (F) saber saw, (G) pad sander, (H) block plane,
(I) sanding block, (J) handsaw,
(K) hacksaw, (L) chisel, and
(M) aviation snips.

Tools & Materials

SAFETY EQUIPMENT

USE SPECIAL EQUIPMENT to protect your body from injury while using power tools. Wear *safety goggles* or plastic glasses when working with power saws. *Ear plugs or earmuffs* protect your hearing. Whichever you use, be sure it has a noise reduction rating (NRR) of at least 20 decibels. Protect your lungs, especially when working with pressure-treated wood. A simple *dust mask* keeps out the sawdust, but use a *respirator* with a replaceable filter when working with toxic products. *Work gloves* help you avoid hand injuries. If you will be on your knees for an hour or more, wear *knee pads*. Have a basic *first-aid kit* on hand so you can clean and cover small cuts and deal with other minor injuries.

Protect yourself with
(A) gloves, (B) ear protection,
(C) hard hat, (D) knee pads,
(E) respirator/dust mask,
(F) safety glasses, (G) work gloves,
and (H) first-aid kit.

CORDLESS TOOL TIPS

CORDLESS DRILLS, drivers, reciprocating saws, and even saber saws all are easier to use on the job site than corded models. For heavy projects, 18-volt tools are recommended. (Cordless circular saws are the exception. Most cordless circular saws are for trim work only and are not suitable for cutting a lot of 2-by lumber.)

The cheapest cordless tools generally perform poorly; you're better off buying mid-priced or more-expensive tools. Often multitool kits are the best value, as long as you really need all the tools in the kit.

Most cordless tools sold today use lithium ion (Li-Io) batteries, which charge faster, stay charged longer, and have a longer lifetime than Nickel metal-halide (NiMH) or Nickel Cadmium (NiCad) batteries. If you have a tool with NiMH or NiCad batteries that have died or need constant recharging, it may be time to switch to a new set of Li-Io tools because new batteries for the old tools will be pricey anyway.

Consider the battery's amp-hour rating, which indicates not only the run time but also the lifetime of the battery. A battery with a three-hour amp-hour rating will obviously last longer than one with a two-hour rating.

Have at least one extra battery on hand, so you can keep one charging while others are being used. Consider buying a model with a quick-charger, which will charge a battery in minutes rather than an hour or more.

Power Nailers

Nowadays builders use *power nailers* for almost all nailing. Though bulky, a power nailer drives nails quickly and sets them at the desired depth. And you can hold boards in position with one hand while driving with the other. For a few hundred bucks you can buy a basic kit that includes the *compressor*, a *framing nailer*, and a *finishing nailer* and/or stapler. Or buy individual cordless nailers, which are powered by fuel cells that must be replaced from time to time.

There are two basic ways to power-drive nails. With im- pact driving, you squeeze the trigger, then "bounce" the nailer's tip onto the surface to activate the power. With trigger driving, you start with your finger off the trigger, press the nailer's tip where you want the nail driven, then squeeze the trigger. For safety, some nailers have mecha- nisms that allow the tool to drive only one way or the other, to prevent accidental nailing.

In addition to a framing and finishing nailer, you may need a *roofing nailer*, which drives large-headed nails impact-style. To attach screening directly to a post, use a wide-crown nailer.

Power nailers. (A) A compressor provides the power; use one with a long air hose; (B) a roofing nailer holds a round clip of roofing nails; (C) a finishing nailer drives finishing brads; (D) use a framing nailer for heavy-duty work.

GO FOR SQUARE DRIVE

THE MOST COMMONLY AVAILABLE SCREWS are Phillips heads, which work fairly well. Be sure to use a Phillips head bit of the right size—usually #2—and change bits when they become worn. But Phillips head bits and screw heads often strip out, making it difficult to finish driving or removing a screw.

For greater grab and fewer frustrations, use square-head screws with an appropriate sized screw head. These almost never strip out.

smart tip

POWER NAILING TIPS

POWER NAILERS CERTAINLY MAKE THE WORK GO FASTER, BUT THEY ARE NOT FOOLPROOF. THE GOAL WITH MOST NAILERS IS TO SEAT THE NAIL FLUSH WITH THE SURFACE OF THE WOOD. TO DO THAT NAIL AFTER NAIL, MAKE SURE THE FORCE OF THE TOOL MATCHES THE DENSITY OF THE WOOD TO SEAT THE NAIL PROPERLY, LEFT. TOO MUCH FORCE CAN RESULT IN SPLITS THAT WILL TRAP WATER, RIGHT.

DRIVERS & DRILLS

MOST PEOPLE ARE COMFORTABLE using a 16-ounce hammer to drive nails manually, but if you've had an extra biscuit for breakfast and want to sink nails faster, consider a 20-ouncer. Choose a hammer that feels comfortable; you'll use it often. To finish driving nails without marring adjacent wood, or to set nails into the wood, use a nail set.

To drive large screws or bolts, you may need a ratchet wrench with the right-size sockets.

The cordless ⅜-inch drill has become the most common tool for boring holes and driving screws. It's far more maneuverable than a corded drill, and most models are nearly as powerful. A 14-volt drill is just strong enough for most jobs; an 18-volt drill will do it all with authority.

In addition to a good set of drill bits, equip your drill with a magnetic sleeve and a variety of small bits that you insert into the sleeve. The magnetic effect makes it easier to place and hold the bit in the screw head.

If codes require you to drive lots of heavy-duty screws, consider renting or buying an impact driver. It's stubbier than a standard drill but provides extra torque for heavy duty driving.

Cordless Drill

Impact Driver

CHOOSING LUMBER

In addition to the lumber used for the deck and framing, you'll need roofing materials, as well as siding for the exterior walls. The next six pages will guide you in choosing not just the correct materials, but the best and longest-lasting materials as well.

Though a porch's floor and undersides are largely protected from the weather, its structure should be built using materials that are very resistant to rot—as though it were a deck. Once you get to the roof, however, standard building materials, such as those used to build a house, are the norm.

Understanding treatment. Older pressure-treated boards were treated with chromated copper arsenate (CCA), which has been banned for most uses because of the harmful effects of arsenate. Today you may find boards treated with a variety of chemicals, including ammoniacal copper quaternary (ACQ), copper borate azole (CBA, or CA-B), and copper azole (CA).

The newer treatments replace the old arsenate with copper, which is somewhat expensive. Less-expensive lumber, with a lower copper content, is generally rated for "aboveground" use. It will resist rot as long as it's not in prolonged contact with moisture. If a board will be sunk in the ground or placed where it sits in moisture, you should pay more for lumber that is rated "ground contact."

While pressure-treated lumber is often used for a porch's framing, more decorative woods serve as porch floors, walls, and ceilings.

TREATED LUMBER

USE TREATED LUMBER for the deck framing and for the posts and headers that make up the walls.

The most important information on a pressure-treated board's sticker is whether the board is approved for ground contact or for aboveground use only.

Pressure-treated lumber can range in color from green to yellow to blond. Newer treatment techniques account for the range of colors. Be sure to check product information sheets for selecting the correct fasteners to use.

Wood species. Different types of lumber work differently with the treatment. Douglas fir is strong and stable, but it doesn't soak up treatment readily. So it has a grid of incisions that are cut to facilitate injection. Southern yellow pine is also strong, but it is a bit brittle and likely to crack. It accepts the treatment easily, so there are no incisions.

The designation "hem-fir" refers to a general grouping of species. In some areas, hem-fir is strong and stable, while in other areas it may warp and crack easily. Check with local builders or your inspector before using it.

Fasteners. The copper in the treatment reacts chemically with some types of galvanized fasteners and flashings, causing them to deteriorate. Use nails, screws, hardware pieces, and flashings that are rated safe for treated lumber. Stainless-steel works well but is expensive. Other "decking" fasteners have an extra polyester coating or stronger galvanizing to prevent reactions.

Gradings. Use No. 2 or better for all structural work. For boards that will show, use Select or No. 1 boards. Boards that are kiln-dried after treatment (and marked KDAT) have a low moisture content, making them both stable and ready to receive stain.

STAINING TREATED WOOD?

YOU CAN PURCHASE STAIN made specifically for treated wood. Basically, it contains extra red pigment to off-set the wood's greenish hue. People disagree widely on the effect of staining treated wood, so experiment with some scrap pieces, or take a look at other porches with stained treated wood to see whether or not you like the look. (To get the full protection and long-lasting color, apply sealer as well as the stain, unless the stain is a one-step product.)

LUMBER GRADING

A STICKER ON THE END of a board, or a stamp on its side, indicates the board's grade. Grading systems can vary depending on the species, but in general:

- **Select, Select Structural, or No. 1** are the highest-quality boards with the fewest defects. They are the most resistant to shrinking, warping, and cracking.
- **No. 2 boards** are the standard choice for framing. They have some knots or other defects, but inspectors consider them strong and stable enough for structural work.
- Avoid using boards rated **No. 3 or Utility.** They are likely to warp and crack and may have defects that compromise their strength.

Plywood

Plywood is made by laminating thin wood plies together with the grain of one ply running perpendicular to the grains of the plies above and below. The result is a very strong product, one that is difficult to crack. Plywood is usually rated according to the quality of the top and bottom plies, with "A" being the highest rating. AB plywood, for instance, has a knot-free A surface on top and a B surface, with only minor defects, on the bottom. "CDX plywood, the most common type used in sheathing, has a C surface, a D surface—the "X" means that it has interior plies made of scraps (and not exterior glue, as is commonly thought).

For sheathing a roof, perhaps the most common choice is ½-inch CDX, which is strong enough to span rafters 16 inches apart. To support a tile floor, it is common to install ¾-inch CDX with a layer of cement backer board on top.

Oriented-strand board (OSB), also called waferboard, is an economical choice. It is made of many wafers of wood, rather than full-size plies. It is strong enough to meet code for roof sheathing in most areas, but it is not as strong as plywood.

Brazilian Hardwoods

Also called tropical hardwoods or ironwoods, this grouping includes ipé (also known as Brazilian walnut), garapa (Brazilian ash), cambara (Brazilian mahogany), and cumaru (Brazilian teak). Terms like "walnut" refer only to the appearance of the wood; the Brazilian versions are not related to those species.

These woods are extremely hard, strong, and durable. When used as the floor for a porch, you will need to stain and finish them only every few years. Tongue-and-groove versions are available, but some people prefer to install them as you would regular decking with small gaps between the boards.

This display shows a number of tropical hardwoods. All have been treated with a plain finish that has only a small amount of stain.

PLYWOOD GRADING

Intended Use of Panel Type

APA
THE ENGINEERED WOOD ASSOCIATION

RATED SHEATHING

Panel Thickness

Maximum Span for Roof Sheathing/ Floor Sheathing

32/16   15/32 INCH

SIZED FOR SPACING
EXPOSURE 1

Exposure Rating

000

Mill Number

PS 1-95   C-D   PRP-108

Grade

This plywood is rated for use as sheathing, and so meets codes for use on a roof. Though it is actually ¹⁵⁄₃₂ in. thick, it is generally referred to as ½ in.

Ironwoods such as ipé are so costly and beautiful that builders sometimes go to the trouble of sinking the screw heads, filling the holes with plugs, and sanding smooth for a handcrafted look.

SAPWOOD, HEARTWOOD, VERTICAL AND FLAT GRAIN

A TREE'S SAPWOOD is located toward the perimeter of the tree and is often relatively light in color. Heartwood, which is usually darker, comes from the center of the tree. Heartwood is denser, more stable, and more resistant to rot. The distinction is especially important when it comes to redwood and cedar: for these species, the heartwood can be very rot resistant, but the sapwood may develop rot in a few years.

Boards with vertical grain have closely spaced, parallel grain lines. Boards with flat grain have wavy, widely spaced grain lines that sometimes form points. Many boards, like the one shown below, display a combination of vertical and flat grain. Wood with vertical grain is more stable and strong. Whenever possible, choose boards with a preponderance of straight, narrow grain lines.

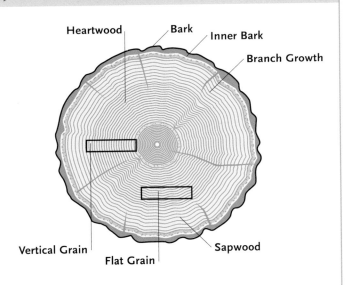

Heartwood · Bark · Inner Bark · Branch Growth · Vertical Grain · Flat Grain · Sapwood

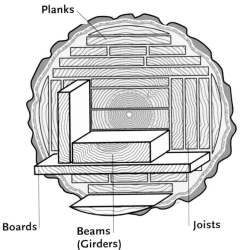

Planks · Boards · Beams (Girders) · Joists

75

Choosing Boards

If possible, take the time to select boards individually. Make a quick visual inspection, checking for the defects shown in the illustration below. It's important to know which defects are structural and which are merely cosmetic.

A *bow* is a bend in the wood along the face, from end to end. As long as it is not severe, you can take out a bow when you install the board. A *cup* is a bend across the width of a board. Minor cupping can sometimes be straightened out as you drive fasteners through the middle of the board. However, if the cupping is severe, it cannot be removed. *Crook*, sometimes called crown, is a bend in the board along its length, visible when you sight along the narrow edge of the board. Most boards have a slight crown; always install joists crown side up. *Twist* is a corkscrew-shaped distortion. A *check* is a rift in the surface of the board; unless it goes deep, it is only a cosmetic problem. A *split* is a crack all the way through a board at its end. Unless you can cut off the split portion, avoid using a board with a split. *Wane* is a lack of wood, and sometimes the presence of bark, along the edge of a board. Unless it is very wide, wane does not affect strength. Small, firm *knots* are only cosmetic flaws, but a knot that is large and loose can affect a board's strength. If you see *decay*—evidence of rot from moisture or insects—do not use the board. *Pitch pockets* are accumulations of sticky resins. They will not affect strength, but will cause discoloration if you stain the board.

LUMBER DEFECTS

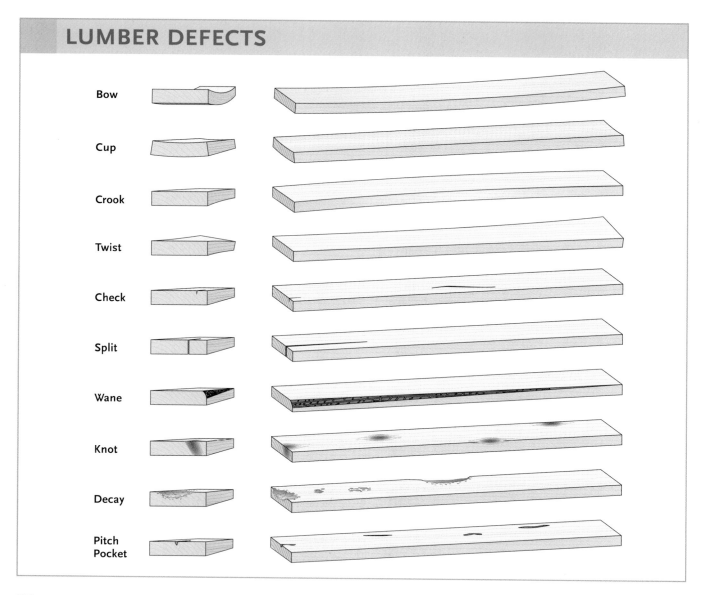

Bow

Cup

Crook

Twist

Check

Split

Wane

Knot

Decay

Pitch Pocket

Composite Decking with Variegated Colors

Composite Decking for Porches

Many types of composite decking have a plain appearance and a rough surface, which may make them unsuitable for a nearly indoor floor. However, composites do offer very easy maintenance—just wipe them down once in awhile. And some higher-end composite and vinyl decking products have attractive faux wood patterns. Some types are available in a tongue-and-groove configuration, to form a gapless surface that does not need to be protected from bugs with underscreening.

Bead-board

Bead-board is a traditional finish for a porch ceiling, and can be used for knee walls as well. Standard bead-board is ¾ inch thick and about 3½ inches wide, with a groove running down its middle. The groove matches the look of the tongue-and-groove joint, so the finished ceiling has a series of grooves spaced about 2 inches apart. Other sizes are available, producing grooves that are closer or farther apart. A variety of groove styles are available as well. Thinner bead-board, ⅜ inch thick, is not recommended unless it can be fastened every 12 inches or so.

If you will stain the wood, choose among pine, fir, and cedar. For a clean look, choose boards that are clear of knots. Knotty boards lend a more rustic appearance. Knotty pine paneling has plenty of knots and widely spaced grooves, suitable for a cabin style.

If you will paint the bead-board, you may choose to install plywood sheets with a faux bead-board pattern. If you want a pure white surface that is nearly maintenance free, consider PVC boards or sheets.

Pine or fir bead-board can be stained, covered with a clear finish, or painted.

CHECK THE CROWN

BEFORE INSTALLING A JOIST
or putting together a laminated beam, sight along the edge of the board to find the crown—the bend along the length of the board. Mark the crown side with an X or an arrow and install the lumber crown side up.

OTHER MATERIALS

A porch employs a variety of materials, many of which are described in following chapters. Here are some of the most common.

Concrete

Use bags of concrete dry mix to make concrete for footings. Unless you have a whole lot of concrete to pour, it is not worth the trouble to mix your own sand, cement, and gravel. Consult with your inspector for the type of concrete that will be strong enough. Standard mix may be fine, or you may be required to use a "high strength" or "high-early" mix.

HIDDEN FASTENERS

MOST PEOPLE PREFER NOT to have exposed nail or screw heads on a porch floor. You can choose among a variety of "hidden" fasteners that will hold decking boards nearly invisibly. Some grab the side of a board using barbs and are fastened to the top of the joist with a screw. Others slip into a groove in the side of the decking board. A continuous fastener runs along the side of the joist, at its top, and is screwed to the joist and to the underside of the decking boards.

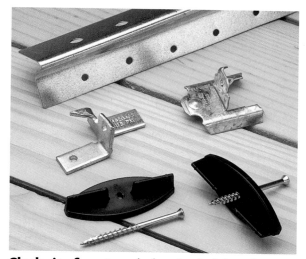

Clockwise from top: deck strip, deck board tie, slot ties, deck clip. With these and other products you don't need any surface nails.

Fasteners

The nails, screws, and bolts you use to join your porch together are sometimes dictated by building codes. In some cases, the choice is yours. In general, a nail or screw should be at least twice as long as the thickness of the piece you are fastening. Use nails and screws approved for use with pressure-treated lumber.

Hand-nailing is still a common method, but power-nailing and driving screws makes the job go faster, is less likely to produce dents in the wood, and creates stronger joints. (For more on the tools used for power attachment of nails and screws, see pages 70–71.)

Nails are sized by the term "penny," abbreviated to the letter "d" (from the ancient Roman coin the denarius). Use 16d nails, which are 3 inches long, to attach 2-by lumber. For ⁵⁄₄ decking (which is 1 inch thick), 10d or 12d nails work best. Screws are simply described according to their lengths.

A quick-drive screw gun, shown below, quickly drives screws attached to a plastic clip, so you don't have to fumble with individual screws while you are working. You can rent a professional model, or buy an inexpensive attachment for a standard drill.

Use bolts or lag screws for very firm attachment of large boards. A j-bolt is inserted into concrete with its threads poking up, so you can attach a post anchor. To attach to brick or concrete, use lag shields and screw or use hammer-driven concrete anchors. (See page 87.)

Quick-drive drill attachments eliminate the need to set each screw individually. Locked into to a standard drill, the attachment feeds decking screws into position so that you can drive one screw after another.

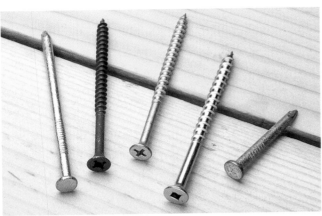

Nails and screws. Left to right: 10d common nail, coated rust-proof deck screw, galvanized Philips-head screw, stainless-steel square-drive screw, joist-hanger nail.

Bolts. Left to right: galvanized lag screw, stainless-steel lag screw, J-bolt, stainless-steel carriage bolt, galvanized carriage bolt, masonry shields.

Fastening Hardware

A variety of specific fasteners are required to keep all the structural parts of a porch in place. Be sure to use the exact fasteners required by the building department. For treated lumber, the fasteners should be rated for use with treated lumber, so they do not cause a chemical reaction and deteriorate. Shown below are some of the more common fasteners. A *post cap* anchors a girder to the top of a post. A *post base* secures the post bottom to the concrete footing. A *joist hanger* holds joists firmly in place against a header or the ledger; use *corner brackets* at corners. Some areas require the use of hurricane or seismic ties.

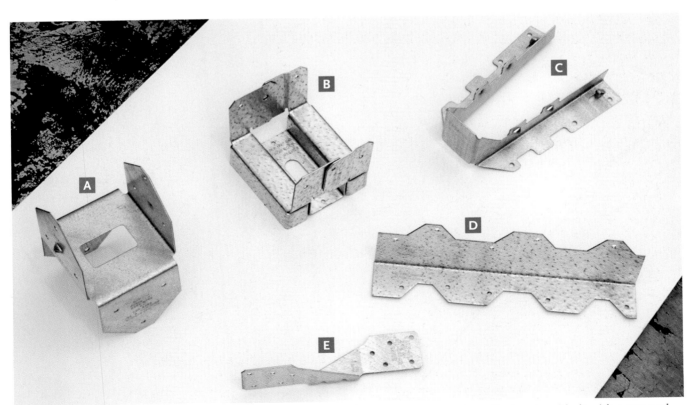

Framing hardware. (A) Post cap attaches beams to the top of posts; (B) post anchor attaches to a j-bolt with a nut and washer and connects a post to its concrete footing; (C) joist hanger; (D) corner bracket; (E) seismic or hurricane tie.

ROOFING AND GUTTERS

A porch roof must be every bit as weather-resistant and durable as the house's roof. In most cases, it is built much the same way, using the same materials.

Sheathing

One-half-inch plywood (often, CDX grade) or oriented-strand board (OSB, also called waferboard) are two common choices for basic roof sheathing. Plywood is stronger than OSB, which costs less but does not meet some local codes. If the ceiling inside will not be covered with bead-board or another finish surface, then the underside of the sheathing will show. In that case it is common practice to install ¾-inch grooved siding with the grooves facing down.

Flashings

Check with your building department to be sure you are using approved flashings along edges and wherever the porch roof meets the house or another surface. Use approved materials, and make sure your flashings are sufficiently wide. If you need a very long piece of flashing, you may choose to bend and form your own, as shown on page 137. For most purposes you can buy preformed flashing pieces that are as long as 8 or 10 feet.

Aluminum is the most common flashing material: it won't rust and is fairly strong, though long pieces can be accidentally bent out of shape. Avoid galvanized flashings, which will rust in time. Vinyl flashing products are popular in some areas; they will not bend like aluminum. If your house has copper flashing, you may want to use copper on the porch as well; you may need to bend your own pieces.

Around the roof edge, install code-approved drip edge flashing. T-shaped drip edge is the most common choice. A wraparound drip edge covers the edge of the sheathing. Eave trim has a simpler profile. On a gable roof, one type of flashing may be called for along the eave edges (the horizontal line at the bottom) and another type for the rake (the angled portions). Where there will be a gutter, make sure the flashing will direct water into it. Where a gable roof meets the house at an angle, use short pieces of step flashing, one per shingle. Where a shed roof meets the house, use a long piece of wall flashing. Both step and wall flashings are simple pieces of bent metal or vinyl.

Various flashings. (A) aluminum roll flashing; (B) step flashing; (C) L-flashing; (D) T-shaped drip edge; (E) wraparound drip edge; (F) angle drip edge.

Ice guard

Roofing felt

Roofing Felt or Ice Guard

Often called tar paper, roofing felt is stapled to the sheathing prior to installing the shingles. Don't neglect the felt; it is critical to keeping the sheathing dry. Fifteen-pound felt meets code in most areas, but 30-pound felt is recommended because it is twice as thick and is less apt to wrinkle during installation.

Ice-guard membrane, also known as waterproofing shingle underlayment (WSU), is a thick sheet that is sticky on one side to adhere to the roof. It seals around nails that are driven through it. In many areas with freezing winters, WSU is required for the bottom portion of a roof to prevent damage from ice damming. If a roof has a low pitch, it is a good idea to install WSU over the entire roof.

SHINGLES

COMPOSITION SHINGLES are the most common finish roofing materials. They are often called asphalt shingles, but true asphalt shingles are not as durable as composition shingles. Fiberglass shingles are also durable, and are common in many areas. Buy shingles rated to last 30 years; you will only save a little money by buying 20-year shingles, and even if you expect to move soon, the longer guarantee will help sell the house.

Most homes are roofed using three-tab shingles. Architectural shingles are thicker and have a rich texture.

If your house is roofed with slate, tile, wood shingles, or another roofing material, consider matching the porch roof with the existing house roof.

GUTTERS AND DOWNSPOUTS

ALUMINUM GUTTERS AND DOWNSPOUTS are inexpensive and not difficult to install. You will need to cut pieces to fit and attach the parts with gutter caulk and pop rivets. Aluminum resists rust but is not very strong; it may bend when a ladder is placed against it. Vinyl components are stronger but a bit more expensive. Some types have rubber seals, while others attach with solvent, much as you would assemble PVC plumbing pipe.

You will need end caps, a drop outlet or two, and downspout sections.

Vinyl components

Aluminum components

SCREENING OPTIONS

Porch screening was once a choice between fiberglass, which tended to warp, and metal, which rusted. Today you have a great variety of screening options, many of which have amazing strength and durability. There is a variety of porch screen and window panels and sashes from which to choose.

Screening Fabrics

Fiberglass is now the near universal choice for screening fabric (also called screen cloth). Aluminum fabric is a distant second; it is not as strong and dents easily. Other materials, such as stainless steel and brass, are expensive and for specialty uses only. A home center will carry a couple of screening fabrics, but for a more varied choice, visit glass stores and online sources. Here are some options to consider:

- Screen fabric comes in various strengths. Some fiberglass "superscreen" fabric is so strong you could walk on it (if it were stretched out horizontally). You'll pay more for stronger fabric, but you won't have to worry about damage due to people accidentally bumping into it.
- A home center will carry rolls up to 3 feet wide, but some stronger fabrics are available in rolls 6 feet or wider.
- Charcoal is the most popular color, but some people prefer gray.
- Mesh size is the number of openings per square inch. The most common choice for porch screening is 18 x 14 mesh (18 openings wide by 14 openings tall per square inch); this will keep out mosquitoes and most other bugs. But if you have no-see-ums or other very tiny insects, 20 x 20 mesh is recommended.
- Some screening is rated according to the amount of sun it blocks. This is determined by the size of the openings and by the reflective properties of the screen material. Screening rated at 50 percent sun blocking provides shade as well as good visibility; screening rated for 90 percent sun blocking is almost like a window shade.
- "One-way" screening is privacy screening. It provides good visibility when looking out from the porch, but the screening makes it difficult for outsiders to see into the porch.

Charcoal-colored fiberglass fabric with a 18 x 14 mesh is the most common screening choice.

THE PORCH DOOR

TRADITIONALLY, porch doors were flimsy wooden screen affairs with stapled-on screening and crude springs that caused them to bang shut. While these have a certain nostalgic charm, they are easily bent out of shape and do not effectively shut out bugs.

Nowadays most builders use security storm-and-screen doors made of sturdy aluminum, steel, or well-joined wood. They come in a variety of styles and colors. A high-quality model is nearly as sturdy and stable as a metal exterior door. And they are called "security" doors for a reason: they have reliable locks and hefty hinges, making them extremely difficult to jimmy open.

At the bottom of the door is an adjustable gasket, which can be moved up and down to seal out insects. It is important to install a threshold in the doorway, so the gasket does not scrape the floor while it swings.

This aluminum porch door is positioned about three feet from the house's sliding door— just enough space for maneuvering in either direction.

SCREEN PANEL CHOICES

A WIDE CHOICE of screen sashes is available from online sources, specialty stores, and local fabricators. Here are some of the most common types.

❚ You can simply stretch heavy-duty screening and staple it to the structural posts. Use wide-crown staples, which are fastened with a pneumatic gun, rather than hand staples. Cover the staples by applying trim boards (left).

❚ To use a two-part channel system (whose parts are shown below), nail the black portion to the post. Stretch the screening across the black piece, and staple it. Attach the light-colored top piece by pressing it into the black piece's grooves; this will secure the screening and tighten it a bit as well.

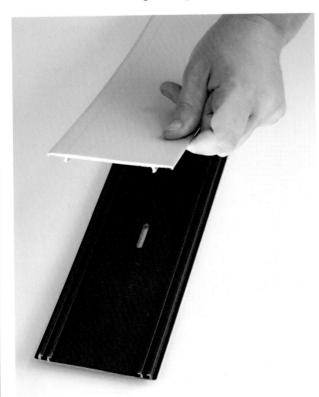

❚ A glass store or a local fabricator can make simple aluminum frames to the dimensions you supply. These units have screws in the inside of the frames to hold them in place. Disadvantages: your measurements must be precise because there is no room for error; you may need to wait a week or more for delivery.

❚ Screen companies sell systems with channels that you cut to fit into the framing. It typically takes a half hour or so to make each screen section. Some use vinyl frames, others use aluminum. Cut and install the outer pieces around the opening. Working with a helper, stretch the screening taut and press it into the frame pieces. Depending on the system, you either press the fabric into grooves with a spline tool, or you simply snap inner pieces in place to finish tightening the screening.

❚ A motorized or hand-crank screen system allows you to raise and lower screening, so you can enjoy full visibility when the bugs are gone and protection when they are around. This is the most expensive option, but you may want to consider it for the window you most often gaze through.

❚ Some companies make what are essentially window units, which combine permanent screens with moveable or removable clear acrylic sashes. (The display sample shown on the right demonstrates four colors of acrylic from which to choose.) Adding or lowering the movable acrylic sashes helps turn a three-season porch into a year-round option.

building 4
the deck

A PORCH MAY BE BUILT using an existing deck or patio as its floor, but most often a new porch requires a new floor. As with house construction, the walls and roof are built on top of the deck. If you are planning on a shed roof or a gable roof with a ridge beam and no rafter ties, then the front edge of the deck will support the roof. On a gable roof with rafter ties, the side edges support the roof.

ATTACHING THE LEDGER

Building a floor for a porch is similar to building an outdoor deck. A ledger attached to the house will support joists for the floor. Install the ledger first so you can measure from it to establish the heights of posts and other framing members. Plan to make the top of the ledger one decking board's thickness below the final surface of the deck; the bottom of the ledger represents the height of girders, or beams.

The ledger should be made of the same material as the joists—usually, 2x8, 2x10 or 2x12 lumber. Because moisture may be trapped between it and the house, you may choose to use treated lumber rated for ground contact rather than lumber rated for aboveground use.

Building codes covering ledger attachment vary greatly, depending on your building department and your type of siding. It may be enough to simply place the ledger against the house and attach with screws. Or you may be required to drive large ½-inch lag screws or even attach the ledger to the house using bolts. Whichever fastener you use, it is important to attach the ledger to the house's rim joist or studs—not just to the sheathing. If you are attaching to masonry, use the masonry anchors specified by codes.

In addition to strength, building departments are also very concerned with moisture infiltration. If you remove the siding to install the ledger, cover the sheathing with self-stick flashing or ice guard or at least roofing felt. Also apply flashing above the ledger to keep water away from the house and the ledger. The flashing should extend at least 3 inches up and under the siding.

LEDGER-LOCK SCREWS

MANY BUILDING DEPARTMENTS now allow—or require—the use of special ¼-inch screws made especially for ledgers rather than ½-inch lag screws. The ledger screws are made of hardened metal, so they are just as strong as the thicker lag screws. And because they are thinner, they allow for less moisture infiltration around their threads. To be really sure that water will not wick along the screws and into the house, drive them at a slight upward angle.

ATTACHING A LEDGER TO A FRAMED WALL

project

Cut wood siding using a circular saw. If you have vinyl or aluminum siding, use the saw or a knife and a straightedge. You will need to pry the siding away from the house and perhaps remove some nails in order to slip the flashing up and under the siding above the ledger.

TOOLS & MATERIALS

▮ Level or water level ▮ Shims
▮ Pry bar ▮ Circular saw ▮ Knife
▮ Chisel ▮ Drill or impact driver

1 Use a water level or a carpenter's level set atop a straight board to mark the height and ends of the ledger. Snap chalk lines.

ATTACHING A LEDGER TO A MASONRY WALL

project

A variety of masonry anchors can attach a ledger firmly to brick, block, or concrete. Here, two anchors are used: gun-driven nails to hold the ledger in place and hammer-driven sleeve anchors. You could also use masonry screws or lag screws with masonry shields.

- Level or water level
- Measuring tape
- Pencil
- Powder-actuated nail gun with nails
- Hammer drill
- Wood and masonry bits
- Hammer
- Hammer-driven anchors

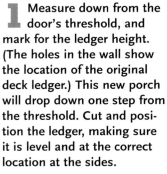

1 Measure down from the door's threshold, and mark for the ledger height. (The holes in the wall show the location of the original deck ledger.) This new porch will drop down one step from the threshold. Cut and position the ledger, making sure it is level and at the correct location at the sides.

2 Use a powder-actuated gun to drive nails through the ledger and into the masonry wall. Load a cap and a nail; press the gun against the wood; and pull the trigger to fire. If the ledger is not perfectly straight, have a helper bend it up or down as needed while you drive nails.

3 Drill holes through the ledger into the masonry. Drill holes about half an inch deeper than the length of the anchors. Slip the anchors into the holes; then use a hammer to drive them tight against the board.

2 Set the circular saw to cut just through the siding and not into the sheathing. Cut along the lines, and finish cuts at the edges using a chisel or aviation snips.

3 Insert code-approved flashing. Cut the ledger to fit, and mark with the locations of the joists. Drive screws as required by your building department.

LAYING OUT AND POURING FOOTINGS

There are a number of ways to install footings and posts. Building codes often specify a specific installation method, so be sure to check before beginning work. Many codes require an in-ground post, as shown here. In other areas, aboveground posts, as shown on the next two pages, are the norm. For a porch with a roof, posts are usually made of 6x6s, but in some cases 4x4 posts may be allowed. Be sure you completely understand how all the framing will be put together before you start digging holes for posts.

UNATTACHED DECK

IN MANY AREAS IT IS ACCEPTABLE to build an unattached porch deck, or floor—although this technique is not as common for porches as it is for decks. Rather than attaching a ledger, install footings, posts, and a girder close to the house, and build the framing an inch or so away from the house with no need to cut into the siding. However, this technique adds to the expense of the project.

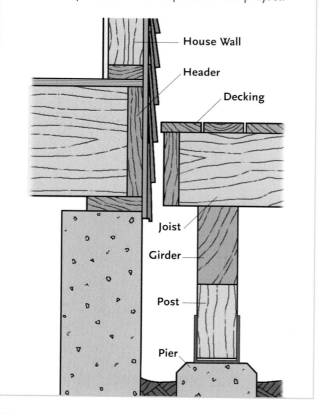

- House Wall
- Header
- Decking
- Joist
- Girder
- Post
- Pier

LAYING OUT

MEASURE OUT FROM THE LEDGER to determine posthole locations. In the example shown below, the joists will cantilever out 16 inches beyond the girder that the posts support. (If there will be no rafter ties and a post will support the roof's ridge beam, then you may not be allowed this sort of cantilever; you may need to position the post directly below the ridge beam.)

Use string lines or long, straight boards to locate the posthole positions. The outside posts must be square to the outside edge of the ledger. To determine square, use the 6-8-10 method, which uses the Pythagorean Theorem you learned in high school and is a good way to determine whether a corner is square. Mark the point on your string line or layout board that is 6 feet from the corner; then mark the ledger 8 feet from the corner. If the distance between the two marks is exactly 10 feet, the layout is square. If not, adjust the string or layout board as needed. The formula is $A^2 + B^2 = C^2$ or in this case $36 + 64 = 100$. The square root of 100 is 10.

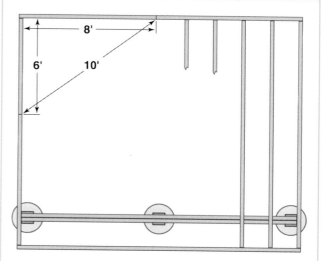

In a typical framing setup, joists cantilever, or run past, the girder, which rests on the posts. At each side, the post is directly beneath the outside joist, so the post's position must be exact. The center post does not have to be in the exact center, but it must be in line with the outside posts so that the girder it supports is straight.

FOOTING OPTIONS

THERE ARE THREE OPTIONS for installing footings and framing:

Lay out the framing, and dig the postholes; then pour the concrete. Install the posts at the correct height. (The front posts will be notched a girder's, or beam's, width below the bottom of the ledger; the girders will support the joists.) Attach the girder to the front posts, and build the rest of the framing.

Lay out the framing, and dig the postholes. Build the framing—the girders and joists—resting on temporary supports. When the framing is complete, pour the concrete, and cut the posts to fit under the girder or joists. Install the posts, and remove the temporary supports.

If the porch's deck is raised high above the ground so that there is plenty of room to work underneath, you can build the framing on long temporary supports. Then reference down from the framing to find the posthole locations; dig the holes; pour the concrete; and cut and install the posts.

SIZING POSTHOLES

DETERMINE THE SIZE HOLE you will need, which depends on the type of post and footing you will install. If you will use a tube form, make the hole about 3 inches wider than the tube form. For an in-ground post, the hole may be 12 or 16 inches in diameter, depending on local codes.

If you live in an area with freezing winters, you will be required to dig several inches below your locale's frost line. Even if you are in a warm climate, you may be required to dig 3 feet or more to ensure a strong footing and post.

Hole-Dug Pier with Form

Hole-Dug Tube Form

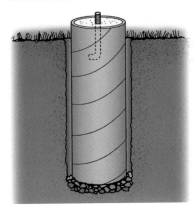

In-Ground Post

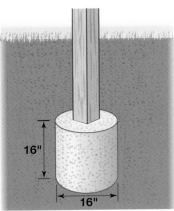

16"

16"

Building the Deck

DIGGING POSTHOLES

DIGGING POSTHOLES may be fairly straightforward if your soil is loose and free of roots. But more often you may need to dig in clay, or you may encounter rocks or roots, and this could turn the job into a major headache. You may simply dig holes using a clamshell-type posthole digger. For faster and more powerful digging, rent a two-person power auger. Clean out the hole with a clamshell-type digger.

When digging only a few postholes, most people turn to the clamshell-type digger. The tool allows you to create holes with relatively straight sides.

When digging many holes or if the soil is full of rocks and tree roots, consider renting a power post-hole auger. This one is a two-person model.

Mixing and Pouring Concrete

Tamp the bottom of the hole with a hand tamper or a post. Some codes may require that you shovel in several inches of gravel and tamp that as well.

Use dry concrete mix that meets or exceeds local codes for strength. Mixes labeled "high early" or "extra strength" cost a bit more but will ensure a firm foundation for your posts. Pour one or two bags of dry concrete mix into a wheelbarrow. Add water, and mix with a hoe or a shovel to achieve a mix that is just pourable. The less water, the stronger the concrete will be, so avoid making a soupy mix.

You can also use the builder's trick of mixing concrete in heavy-duty plastic sheeting. Dump the concrete mix onto the sheeting; add water; and slosh and squeeze until the concrete is mostly mixed. Pour the mix into the hole; then poke with a board or rod to complete mixing.

If you will install in-ground posts, pour concrete directly into the hole to the required depth. Allow the concrete to set for at least a day before setting the post on top.

smart tip

HIRE DIGGERS

IF DIGGING IS DIFFICULT, CONSIDER HIRING A LOCAL FENCE OR LANDSCAPING COMPANY TO DIG THE HOLES FOR YOU. THEY WILL HAVE A LARGE POWER AUGER THAT CAN SLICE THROUGH THE SOIL IN SECONDS. BE SURE TO HAVE THE POST LOCATIONS CLEARLY MARKED BEFORE THEY ARRIVE, AND PROVIDE PLENTY OF ACCESS FOR THEIR MACHINERY.

Building the Deck

POURING RAISED FOOTINGS

Some building departments call for concrete footings that rise above grade. Usually this is done using fiberboard concrete tube forms, which create a neat cylinder of concrete. Local codes will specify how large in diameter the tube form should be, as well as the type of post anchor hardware to use.

TOOLS & MATERIALS
- Clamshell digger ▪ Form tubes ▪ Level
- Gravel ▪ Concrete ▪ Trowel
- Post anchor hardware ▪ Wrenches

1 Dig holes to the required depth, and shovel 2–3 in. of gravel into the bottom of the hole. Use a circular saw to cut the tube form to the desired height—in this case, about 6 in. above grade.

2 Check the layout again, to be sure a post centered over the form will end up in the right location. Level the tube, and backfill with soil to hold the tube steady.

3 Mix the concrete according to package directions. Most people use a wheelbarrow for mixing, but some pro porch builders mix the ingredients in a plastic bag.

4 Use a bucket or shovel to pour the concrete into the form. Once you reach the top, insert the J-bolt that comes with the post anchoring hardware into the center of the form. Use a trowel to level the top of the footing.

5 Allow the concrete to cure for at least a day. Attach the rest of the post anchor hardware. Set the post into the hardware, and measure for cutting it to height as explained on the following pages.

Building the Deck

FRAMING THE DECK

The projects on the following pages show the most common post arrangement for a porch with a roof: notched 6x6 posts that support a girder made of two 2-bys. In some cases 4x4 posts with a girder set on top may be allowed.

Measuring and Cutting the Posts

Set a corner post, longer than it needs to be, in place on the concrete footing. Use a level (atop a long, straight board), a water level, or a transit to determine where to cut the post to height. For a 6x6 post, cut a notch for the girder. As shown in the illustration at right, the bottom of the ledger is level with the top of the girder; the bottom of the post notch equals the width of the girder. Cut the top of the post an inch or so short of the top of the girder to make sure it does not get in the way.

Use an angle square and pencil to mark for a notch that will support the girder. If the girder is a doubled 2-by, then the notch should be 3 inches deep. Cut the girder notch first using a circular saw, then a reciprocating saw or handsaw. Set the post in place, and check that the bottom of the notch is at the correct height. Do the same for the other corner post and for any intermediate posts.

EVERYTHING LINES UP

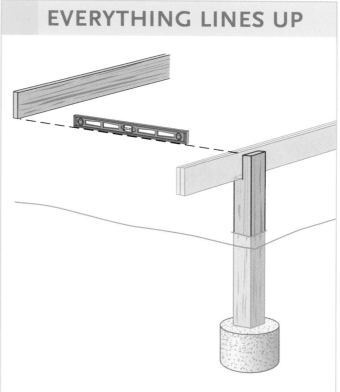

To determine the height of the post, the top of the girder should be level with the bottom of the ledger. Use a water level or a 4-ft. level placed on a long, straight board to check your measurement. For a girder made from double 2-bys, cut the notch 3 in. deep.

CONTINUOUS FOOTING

IN SOME CASES—as when you will have a solid wall under the porch's deck—it makes sense to install a continuous footing. Hire a concrete company to pour the footing. Be sure they pour at the correct height for your walls, and that they place threaded bolts in the correct places so you can anchor the bottom plate.

Allow the concrete to set firmly. Drill holes in the sill plates for the bolts. Slip the boards over the bolts; add washers; and tighten nuts to secure the plates. Once the plate is attached, you can build onto it with a stud wall, posts, or as shown, a rim joist.

1 Continuous footing consists of concrete poured around the perimeter of the porch footprint.

Adding the Girder

Temporarily brace the posts so that they are plumb. Cut the girder boards to length. If the porch is rectangular, they will be the same length as the ledger. Lay one board on top of the other; making sure their crowns are facing the same direction. Drive a grid of nails or screws to laminate the boards together securely.

Place the girder into the notches, and check the layout: the ends of the girder should be square to the ends of the ledger, and the top of the girder should be level with the bottom of the ledger. When you are satisfied, drive screws or nails to anchor the girder to the posts. Drill holes, and fasten the girder securely to the posts using carriage bolts or lag screws, as directed by your inspector.

Continually check for plumb and level as you work, right. Hold the girder in place using screws or nails. Finish the job by securing with carriage bolts or lag screws.

2 Threaded bolts embedded in the concrete anchor the bottom plate in position.

3 Attach the rim joists to the bottom plate to begin framing the floor of the porch.

Building the Deck

INSTALLING JOISTS

project

The joists should be the same dimension lumber as the ledger. In the porch shown here, the end (or side) joists are doubled and reinforced with a footing and post because they will support the roof. The header joist is not doubled and is allowed to cantilever past the girder because it does not support the roof. Mark the ledger and the girder to indicate the locations of the joists, which are typically 16 or 12 inches apart. Draw an "X" to indicate the side of the lines where you will place the joists.

TOOLS & MATERIALS
▌ Code-approved joists
▌ Joist hangers ▌ Hammer and power nailer
▌ Nails and screws ▌ Measuring tape
▌ Circular saw ▌ Square
▌ Chalk line

1 Install the doubled outside joists first. A notched post supports the outside joists in the same way that posts support the girder. Drive screws or nails at an angle to attach the outside joists to the girder and to the ledger.

4 Measure and mark the end joists at the porch's correct distance from the house. Snap a chalk line between the two marks to make a line on top of each joist (inset). Use a square to mark each joist for a square cut.

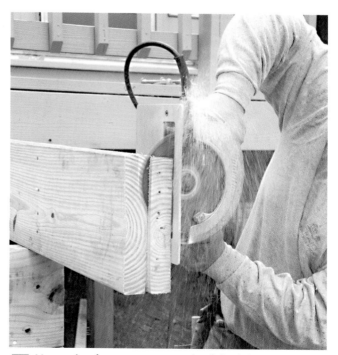

5 Use a circular saw to cut each of the joists square. Position yourself comfortably so that you can make accurate cuts. At the doubled end joists you will need to cut each side.

94

2 Rest one end of each interior joist on the girder. Secure the other end to the ledger temporarily by driving toenails. Slip on joist hangers; tap the hanger's tabs to hold it in place; then drive nails or screws through the holes and into the ledger and the joist (inset).

3 At the girder, align each joist with the layout line that corresponds to the line on the ledger. Drive toenails to fasten the joists to the girder. In some locales you may be required to install hurricane ties at this joint.

6 Position the header joist, crown-side-up, against the joist ends. Drive nails to attach the header to each of the joists; then reinforce by driving screws.

ADDING BLOCKING

Some codes require that you stiffen the joists by adding blocking or bridging. Cut blocking pieces from joist stock, and install them snugly between the joists, driving nails or screws to hold the blocking firmly in place.

Building the Deck

INSTALLING DECKING

We use the word "decking" here, but the word "flooring" could just as well apply because a porch's floor is often protected from the elements and is usually a more finished-looking surface than that on a deck. Tongue-and-groove mahogany decking, shown here, has a tight, straight grain. Mahogany is fairly hard, but ironwoods, such as ipé, are even harder. To install them, you may need to drill holes and drive screws. Check with the building inspector about any flashing requirements.

TOOLS & MATERIALS

- Tongue-and-groove flooring ▮ Measuring tape
- Pencil ▮ Chalk line ▮ Power miter saw
- Large amount of waterproof wood glue
- Pneumatic flooring nailer ▮ Finishing nailer
- Circular saw

1 Place a long, straight piece of decking (you may need two or more to make up the total length against the house.) At each end, mark the top of the outside joist to indicate the width of the board. Snap a chalk line between the two marks (inset).

5 Once you have enough room, switch to the flooring nailer. Hold the nailer with its base pressed against the board being fastened, and hit it with a mallet or hammer.

6 Where a board needs to be bent for a tight fit, have a helper push hard against it. If that doesn't work, drive a chisel into the joist and pry the board into place.

7 Stagger the joints so that you never have two joints right next to each other. For a professional appearance, stagger so there is no place where every other joint is on the same joist.

Building the Deck

2 Measure for cutting boards for the first two or three courses. Boards should meet in the middle of joists. Cut the boards using a power miter saw. Let the boards run wild past the outside joists.

3 Once you have cut the boards and they are ready to be installed, apply wood glue to the tops of the joists. (Not all builders apply glue, but it does make for a firmer connection and reduces squeaking.)

4 Align the first course of boards, tongue side out, with the chalk line. Use a finishing nailer to face-nail these boards. Because space will be too tight to use a flooring nailer, face-nail a second course of boards.

8 Face-nail the last board, which may overhang the framing. Snap a chalk line on top directly above the header, and cut the flooring flush with the header.

9 Also make a chalk-line cut at the sides. The gaps seen here will be covered by the wall framing base plate and the trim.

framing 5 walls & roofs

ONCE THE DECKING IS IN PLACE, you can build the walls. A porch's walls are made of widely spaced posts, most often 4x4s but sometimes 6x6s. The posts are topped with a beam strong enough to span between the posts while supporting the roof rafters. Wall framing is straightforward, but planning a roof and cutting rafters can be complicated, especially on a gable roof. This chapter shows the basics of roof and rafter construction; hire a professional carpenter if you feel out of your depth.

BUILDING PORCH WALLS

Plan for posts that are as consistently spaced as possible for a neat appearance. Space them no farther apart than is allowed by local codes. Make sure any screening or screen/window systems will fit between the posts.

Even if they will be clad with trim, posts will largely determine the look of the porch. Buy posts that are straight; you won't be able to straighten them while building. Posts should be number-one grade or better and dry so that they won't twist or warp. If the frame will not be completely covered with siding, use boards that you won't mind looking at for years—with few cracks and other defects.

When building a wall, take the time to repeatedly check and recheck for level, plumb, straightness, and tight joints. It's OK to end up with minor flaws—say, walls that are out of plumb by ¼ inch or so. But if you start out with even small imperfections, they will tend to multiply as you proceed, so aim for perfection. If the deck is out of level, use shims to level the bottom plate.

Unless you are very skilled with a circular saw, cut all pieces with a power miter saw, and check all pieces to be sure they are cut precisely.

This roof has no rafter ties, so there must be a central post to support the roof's ridge beam.

BUILDING WALLS

project

These steps show building to support a roof with rafter ties, so there is no need for a center post to support the ridge beam. If you will have no rafter ties, be sure to centrally position a post so it supports the ridge beam.

A common porch wall arrangement uses 4x4 posts, 2x4 bottom plate, and 1x4 top plate. (Later, you'll build a beam to rest on top of the top plate.) Your building department may specify different dimensions for the lumber.

TOOLS & MATERIALS

▌Measuring tape ▌Chalk-line box ▌Level ▌Pencil ▌Angle square ▌2x4 and 1x4 plates ▌4x4 posts ▌2x4s for braces ▌Power miter saw ▌Nail gun or hammer ▌Drill ▌Framing nails or screws

3 Where the porch wall will abut the house, hold a level against the siding to check that you can install posts that are plumb. If not, you may need to move the bottom plate (and the wall), rip-cut or trim a post, or remove some siding pieces so that the post you install will be plumb.

1 At each corner of the porch deck, mark spots 3½ in. from the outside of the framing, indicating where the inside of the 2x4 plates will be. Snap chalk lines between the marks.

2 Cut 2x4 bottom plates, and lay them in position on the deck. Parallel plates should be equal in length. Check the corners for square using a framing square. You can also measure the distances between diagonal corners. If they are equal, the layout is square.

4 Use a measuring tape and an angle square to lay out the post positions. Mark for both sides of each post, and draw an X between the marks. Double-check all the post positions for accuracy. Be sure that any doors or windows you plan to install will fit between the posts.

5 Cut top plates (1x4s in this example) to the same lengths as the bottom plates. Place them on top of the bottom plates, and mark them for the positions of the posts as well.

Continued on next page.

Continued from previous page.

6 Cut posts to the height of the walls, minus the thicknesses of the top and bottom plate and the width of the beam. If they will be visible, cut off as many flaws as possible. If they will be covered with trim on the outside only, mark the most flawed sides so that you can position them where they will be covered.

7 Lay out the plates and posts on the deck, and position the post ends inside the Xs you have drawn. (The top sides of the posts and the plate edges will end up facing outward.) At each joint, check to ensure that the post's face is flush with the edge of the plate and correctly positioned. Drive four or more nails to fasten.

10 Once you are certain that the wall is aligned with the chalk line, the end line, and perhaps a wall, drive nails through the bottom plate and into framing—not just into decking.

11 Build, raise, and fasten the other walls in the same way. You may want to attach temporary bracing to the walls as you work, but actually the nails driven through the bottom plate hold surprisingly well, unless it is a windy day.

8 Working with at least one helper, raise the wall into position.

9 Gently nudge the assembly so that it aligns with the chalk lines snapped earlier. If there is a post against the house, check that it is plumb on the side that meets the house.

12 Check posts for plumb, and drive only a few screws to hold them in place. Working with a helper, attach one end of an angled brace; check for plumb; then attach the other end. Attach two braces at each corner.

13 Attach braces near the house as well. Again, check for plumb as you work.

FRAMING A PORCH WITH ANGLES

If the deck has a partial octagon shape with modified corners, framing is a bit more complicated. Snap chalk lines to mark the inside edges of the framing, and plan spacing of posts as for a rectangular porch. Carefully measure and snap chalk lines 3½ inches in from the outside of the framing. Measure two or more sides, to be sure all the pieces (especially the short ones) are the same length.

TOOLS & MATERIALS

▪ Measuring tape ▪ Chalk-line box ▪ 4x4 posts ▪ 2x4 and 1x4 plates ▪ Power miter saw ▪ 2x4s for braces ▪ Level ▪ Pencil ▪ Angle square ▪ Nail gun or hammer ▪ Drill-driver ▪ Framing nails or screws

1 Measure to the inside corners of the chalk lines, and cut the bottom plates at 22½-deg. angles. Cut top plates to match. Place the plates where they will go, and set short pieces of 4x4 at the corners, as shown.

CUTTING SIDING

IF THE HOUSE SIDING INTRUDES and keeps a post from being plumb, you can modify the siding. Here, the inside corner piece on the vinyl siding was getting in the way, so it was removed using a grinder. Finish the cuts with a knife or a hammer and chisel.

smart tip

MARK BOTH PLATES

CUT BOTH THE TOP AND BOTTOM PLATES TO THE SAME LENGTH. HOLD THEM TOGETHER AND MARK BOTH FOR THE POSITIONS OF THE POSTS.

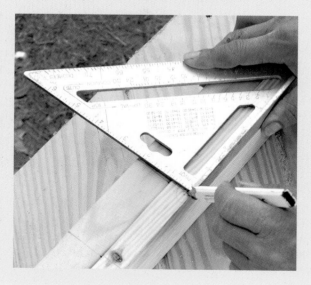

2 Measure from the small posts to lay out the positions of the other posts.

3 Build the walls in order, rather than building the long ones first and then filling in with smaller ones. Build and raise the first wall; check it for alignment; and attach the bottom plate with nails (inset).

4 Build the small wall, which has only two posts. Set the bottom plate for the next wall in place, and align the first wall with it. Drive only a few screws or nails to attach the bottom plate and to tie the two walls together.

5 Add the remaining walls, checking for plumb and correct alignment as you go. Angle-drive screws at the top of the posts to attach the walls together.

ADDING THE BEAM

The top of the wall is capped with a box beam. It is best to construct the beam on-site using 2-by lumber with a ½-inch space between the boards. This will provide plenty of strength for the assembly. For extra stiffness, you could laminate strips of ½-inch treated plywood between the two pieces. Start by installing the outside section of the beam. Note how the corners fit together as shown at right in step 1.

TOOLS & MATERIALS

- 2-by beam pieces ■ 1x4 or 2x4 top plate
- Tape measure ■ Angle square
- Nail gun ■ Drill ■ Nails or screws
- Power miter saw

1 Measure and cut beam pieces that interlock at corners as shown, with ½-in. gaps between. One outside piece comes all the way to the edge; the other is 1½ in. shorter. On the inside, one piece comes to the inside corner, and the other runs 2 in. longer to meet against an outside piece.

FITTING A BEAM AGAINST THE HOUSE

YOU COULD SIMPLY BUTT A STRAIGHT-CUT BEAM PIECE against the house's siding and cover the joint with small trim pieces. Or for a more professional-looking job, take the time to match the beam to the siding. Cut out a cardboard template, the same width as the board, and check for a tight fit (near right). Working on a board that is longer than it needs to be, place the template on the edge of the board and trace the cut line. Cut using a saber saw. Hold the board in place against the siding, and mark for cutting the other end (far right).

2 Start by installing all the outside sections of the beam boards. Cut the boards as you go to fit together as shown in step 1. Work with a helper or two to hold the pieces in position as you work.

3 Hold the first piece flush with the edge of the top plate, and drive screws or nails up through the top plate to hold it in place. It often helps to use a clamp to hold the beam piece tight to the plate.

4 Install the boards for the side, or long, walls; then measure and cut a board to fit snugly between them for the front wall. Check corners for square; then drive nails at the edges to tie the boards together.

5 Install the inside portion of the beam in the same way. Top the beam with cap plates, here made of 1x4s, and nail the assembly together.

UNDERSTANDING ROOF FRAMING

Porch roofs are supported with rafters, which run at an angle and rest on the top of the wall at the lower end and a ridgeboard at the peak. The rafters may be 2-by boards spaced 16 or 24 inches apart or they may be larger 4-by "timbers," which may be spaced farther apart.

Sizing Rafter Boards. The required size of the rafter boards—whether they should be 2x8s or 2x10s, for example—depends on three things.

- **Rafter span.** The longer a rafter must span, the stronger and wider it must be.
- **Roof slope.** The lower the roof's slope (that is, the closer to level), the greater the strain placed on the rafters. A roof with a lower slope may need wider rafters than one with a steeper slope.
- **Rafter spacing.** The distance between rafters affects the size of the rafters. Rafters spaced 24 inches on center take on more load than those spaced 16 inches on center, and so may need to be larger. Grade of lumber may also affect sizing, though most codes call for no. 2 Douglas fir or better.

Slope and Pitch. The terms "slope" and "pitch" are often used interchangeably, but they mean different things.

Slope describes the rafter's vertical rise in inches, or unit rise, per 12 inches of horizontal run, or unit run. If a roof rises 4 inches for every 12 inches, it is described as having a "four twelve" slope, which may be written as 4:12 or 4-in-12. On many elevation drawings of roofs, you'll see a right triangle off to the side that identifies the roof slope, with a 12 at the top and the rise number at the other end. The higher the number of inches in unit rise, the steeper the roof. For instance, an 8-in-12 roof rises 8 inches for every foot of run.

Pitch is the angle of a roof as a ratio of total rise to span. The total rise is the distance between the roof ridge and the top of the top plate of an end wall at the wall's mid-point; the span is the distance from end wall to end wall.

Figuring Total Rise. If you know the slope of a roof you can figure its total rise—its final height. (This is often necessary information when building a porch because the roof's peak cannot be higher than the bottom of a house window.) Divide the total span—from sidewall to side-wall—in half to get the total run. For instance, if your porch has a span of 20 feet, the total run is 10 feet. Now multiply the unit rise by the number of feet in the total run. A 4-in-

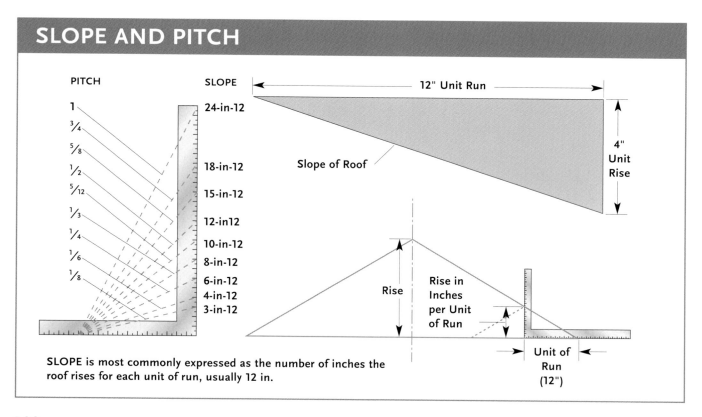

SLOPE AND PITCH

PITCH
1
3/4
5/8
1/2
5/12
1/3
1/4
1/6
1/8

SLOPE
24-in-12
18-in-12
15-in-12
12-in12
10-in-12
8-in-12
6-in-12
4-in-12
3-in-12

12" Unit Run

Slope of Roof

4" Unit Rise

Rise

Rise in Inches per Unit of Run

Unit of Run (12")

SLOPE is most commonly expressed as the number of inches the roof rises for each unit of run, usually 12 in.

12 roof with a total run of 10 feet has a total rise of 40 inches (4 x 10). If you have a 12-foot run with an 8-in-12 roof, the total rise is 96 inches (8 x 12).

When framing a roof, it's important to know the precise rise. When you determine rise, you use a measurement along a line (the measuring line) from the top outside edge of the wall's cap plate to the ridge's centerline. The point at which the rafter measuring line and the ridgeboard centerline intersect is known as the theoretical ridgeboard height. The rise is the distance from the cap plate to the theoretical ridgeboard height.

To determine the inside height of the ridgeboard, or the height at the bottom of the ridgeboard above the cap plate, remember that rafters must have a notch called the bird's-mouth cut so that it sits securely on the cap plate. On a 3½-inch-wide wall, the bird's-mouth cut is about 3¾ inches long horizontally and about 1¾ inches long vertically (depending on your slope).

WILL IT HIT A WINDOW?

AT THE HOUSE, measure and mark the spot in the center—halfway between the two walls—and at the height of the wall's cap plate. Calculate the height of your rafters, as discussed on these pages. Measure up from the mark to determine the height of the rafters. Remember that the finished roof—after sheathing and roofing are installed—will be 2 to 3 inches higher. If the roof will block the window, you will need to lower the roof's slope.

RISE

FIGURING THE TOTAL RISE. Total rise is the vertical measurement from the cap plate to the theoretical ridge height. To find the rise in feet, multiply the run by the unit rise and divide by 12.

Centerline of Ridge

Theoretical Ridge Height

Total Rise

Total Run

FIGURING RAFTERS

Because all the common rafters on a simple gable or shed roof are identical, it's easiest to mark and cut one, and hold it in place to be sure it nests snugly against the ridge board and the wall plate. Once you are certain the first one fits perfectly, use it as a template, or pattern, for marking all the others.

How Many Rafters? If your plan drawing does not indicate all the rafters, use these simple calculations to figure how many you need:

- For rafters that are 16 inches on center, multiply the length of the porch (that is, the length of the ridge board) by three-quarters and add 1 (L x 0.75 + 1 = number of rafters).
- If rafters will be 24 inches on center, multiply the building length by one-half and add 1 (L x 0.5 + 1 = number of rafters)

Three Crucial Cuts. Most rafters have three cuts: the ridge cut, where the rafter rests against the ridgeboard; the birds-mouth cut, where you notch the rafter to sit on the cap plate, and the tail cut, at the end of the rafter. The tail cut may be plumb or square, depending on the desired eave appearance. In most cases, the overhang created by the eave should be at least 12 inches.

Estimating Using a Square. Before you do any serious calculating, estimate the rafter length to make sure you don't go far wrong. Let the long arm of a framing square represent the total run and the narrow arm represent the total rise. Using a scale of 1 inch = 1 foot, measure the distance from the blade to the tongue to find the length of the rafter. On the long arm, add in the overhang as discussed on the next page.

DECIMALS OF A FOOT

DECIMAL	INCH
0.0000	0
0.0052	$^1/_{16}$
0.0104	$^1/_8$
0.015625	$^3/_{16}$
0.0208	$^1/_4$
0.0260	$^5/_{16}$
0.03125	$^3/_8$
0.0365	$^7/_{16}$
0.0417	$^1/_2$
0.046875	$^9/_{16}$
0.0521	$^5/_8$
0.0573	$^{11}/_{16}$
0.0625	$^3/_4$
0.0677	$^{13}/_{16}$
0.0729	$^7/_8$
0.078125	$^{13}/_{16}$

THREE CRUCIAL CUTS

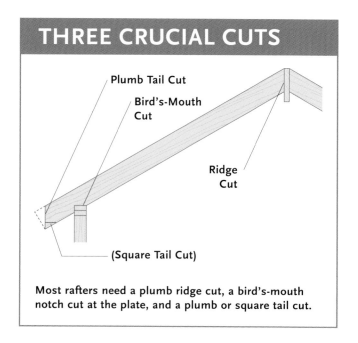

Most rafters need a plumb ridge cut, a bird's-mouth notch cut at the plate, and a plumb or square tail cut.

RAFTER LENGTH

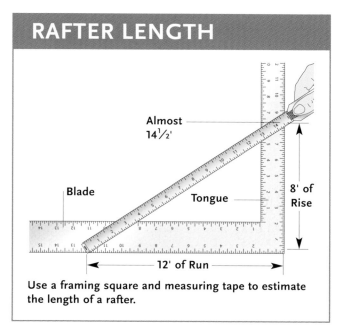

Use a framing square and measuring tape to estimate the length of a rafter.

USING A RAFTER TABLE

BETTER FRAMING SQUARES have a rafter table that contains valuable information for making rafter calculations.

Using a Rafter Table. A framing square gives unit rafter length, to figure gable and shed rafters. Unit length is the common rafter length required, in inches and decimals, at any given slope to gain a foot of run (horizontal distance). A rafter at a steep 10-in-12 slope, for example, has to be longer to cover a foot of run than a rafter at a less-steep 4-in-12 slope.

To find the unit length you need, look on the first line of the wide blade below the inch designation that corresponds to your slope. If, for example, you're framing a 6-in-12 roof, look at the number below the 6-inch mark. You'll find it reads 13.42.

If your total run is 14, multiply 13.42 by 14 to get 187.88 inches. For roof framing, it's usually fine to round off to the nearest 1/8 inch. To be more precise, convert decimals into fractions of inches using the table opposite.

Create an Overhang. The rafter length is the distance from the ridge to the edge of the building. To create an overhang, you need to add extra rafter length beyond the building line. The overhang is a level dimension from the edge of the building, but the actual rafter length is longer because of its slope. If you want an 18-inch, or 1.5 foot, overhang on a 6-in-12 roof, for example, multiply 1.5 x 13.42. The result is 20.13. Divide 20.13 by 12 to get 1.68 feet, or 1 foot 8³⁄₁₆ inches. This is

USING A RAFTER TABLE. Better framing squares have a rafter table that contains valuable information for making rafter calculations.

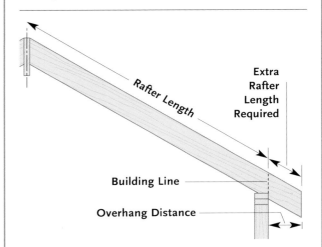

CREATE AN OVERHANG. An overhang is a level dimension from the edge of a building, but you need more rafter length than overhang width because of the slope.

the distance to add along the top edge of the rafter beyond the building line to yield an 18-inch overhang.

smart tip

USING A CONSTRUCTION CALCULATOR

A CALCULATOR MADE SPECIFICALLY FOR THE CONSTRUCTION TRADES QUICKLY FIGURES RAFTER LENGTHS. BE SURE TO BUY ONE THAT WILL DO RAFTER CALCULATIONS; SOME INEXPENSIVE MODELS WILL NOT. TO FIGURE THE LENGTH OF A RAFTER ON A MODEL LIKE THIS ONE, PRESS "PITCH," THEN "INCHES," FOLLOWED BY THE NUMBER OF INCHES PER 12-INCH RISE (FOR EXAMPLE, "5" FOR A 5-IN-12 SLOPE). THEN PRESS "RUN," THEN "FEET" OR "INCHES" FOLLOWED BY THE NUMBER OF FEET OR INCHES. THEN PRESS "DIAGONAL" TO LEARN THE LENGTH OF THE RAFTER.

CUTTING AND INSTALLING A RIDGEBOARD AND RAFTERS

After calculating, use common sense, visualization, and in-place testing to make sure your rafters will fit snugly, especially where they meet the ridgeboard. To mark for a plumb cut, place the framing square on the board with the rise on the narrow tongue and the run on the wide blade.

Mark the Ridge Cut. You have calculated the length of the rafter to the center of the ridgeboard. Now shorten the rafter to accommodate half the thickness of the ridgeboard. For a 2-by ridgeboard, subtract $3/4$ inch.

Determine Rafter Length. Measure from the original ridge line, not the cut line, to the building line. Do not include the overhang. Measure along the top, or crowned, edge of the rafter. Set the framing square at the proper slope; position it at the length mark; and draw a plumb line like the line drawn at the ridge. This is the building line. Add the overhang length, and mark.

Mark the Bird's-Mouth Cut. The plumb portion of the bird's-mouth cut must not exceed one-third the depth of the rafter. Because of the angle of the rafter, the seat portion is generally $3/4$ inch longer than the actual width of the plate it will rest on—$3^3/4$ inches to rest on a 2-by plate. (The steeper the angle, the longer the seat cut, but it is not usually necessary to do calculations to get this precisely right.) Place the framing square with the tongue along the plumb line, and slide the blade until it reads the correct seat length, and mark for the seat cut.

MARKING THE RAFTER

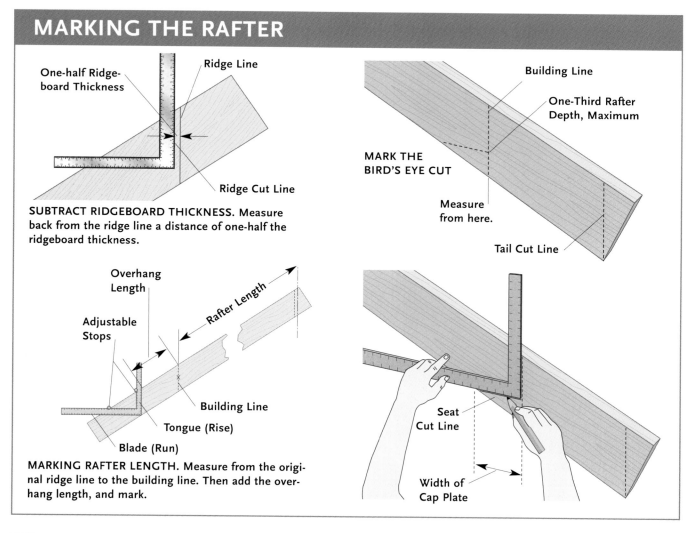

One-half Ridge-board Thickness
Ridge Line
Ridge Cut Line

SUBTRACT RIDGEBOARD THICKNESS. Measure back from the ridge line a distance of one-half the ridgeboard thickness.

Overhang Length
Rafter Length
Adjustable Stops
Building Line
Tongue (Rise)
Blade (Run)

MARKING RAFTER LENGTH. Measure from the original ridge line to the building line. Then add the overhang length, and mark.

Building Line
One-Third Rafter Depth, Maximum
MARK THE BIRD'S EYE CUT
Measure from here.
Tail Cut Line

Seat Cut Line
Width of Cap Plate

CUTTING AND INSTALLING RAFTERS

You'll need two helpers to raise the rafters and the ridgeboard, to check for accurate cuts, and to hold them in place while fastening. Also have on hand plenty of long 2-bys to use for temporary bracing. Hand nailing is possible, but it is much easier to use a power nailer or two.

TOOLS & MATERIALS

▌ Measuring tape ▌ Pencil ▌ Boards for the ridgeboard and rafters ▌ Framing square ▌ Framing calculator ▌ Circular saw ▌ Saber saw or hand saw ▌ 2-bys for temporary bracing ▌ Power nailer and nails

1 Measure across the top caps for the total run in several locations. The walls will probably not be perfectly straight, but you can straighten out minor variations when you install the rafters.

2 Measure the length of the porch (perpendicular to the house), and cut the ridgeboard. In this design, the ridgeboard juts out 3 ft. beyond the front of the porch with an angled section. (See page 120.)

3 Following the instructions on pages 110–112, calculate rafter length and mark for the cuts. Be sure the rafters will be positioned with the crown side up. Make the ridgeline cut first; then measure for the other cuts.

Continued on next page.

Continued from previous page.

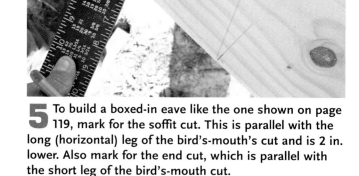

4 For a rafter that will rest on a 3½-in.-wide plate, make the seat of the bird's-mouth cut 3¾ in. long. (The long portion of this line will not be cut.)

5 To build a boxed-in eave like the one shown on page 119, mark for the soffit cut. This is parallel with the long (horizontal) leg of the bird's-mouth's cut and is 2 in. lower. Also mark for the end cut, which is parallel with the short leg of the bird's-mouth cut.

smart tip

PLAN FOR THE SOFFIT AND FASCIA

WHEN CUTTING FOR A BOXED-IN EAVE, TAKE INTO ACCOUNT THE WIDTHS OF YOUR SOFFIT AND FASCIA BOARDS, BUT YOU DO HAVE SOME WIGGLE ROOM. AS SHOWN HERE, THE SOFFIT BOARD DOES NOT NEED TO COME TIGHT TO THE EDGE OF THE WALL, BECAUSE THAT JOINT WILL BE COVERED BY TRIM. AND THE FASCIA CAN HANG DOWN BELOW THE SOFFIT.

8 Working with two helpers, position a rafter near the house, resting it on the top plate at the lower end. Raise the upper end, and use a torpedo level to check the cut angle. When you are satisfied, temporarily nail the rafter to a vertical brace, and drive one or two nails at the bird's mouth. Anchor the brace so it is fairly solid. Do the same for another rafter near the front of the porch.

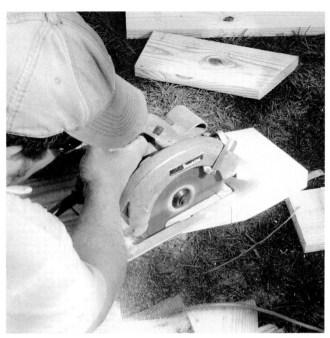

6 Make the cuts. Cut the bird's-mouth notch with a circular saw; then finish with a handsaw. If the cuts will be covered with eave trim later, it's OK to run the circular saw an inch or so past the cut lines—doing so will not weaken the rafter. Cut three rafters.

7 Draw layout lines on the top caps of the walls that indicate the positions of the rafters. If you will sheath the roof with plywood, be sure the ends of the plywood sheets will fall in the centers of the rafters.

9 Draw layout lines on the ridge, indicating where the rafters will go. Attach three or more temporary blocks on top of the ridgeboard. These help keep the rafters in place as you install them.

10 Raise the ridgeboard, with the temporary blocks attached. Temporarily secure it at the correct height by attaching it to a pair of vertical boards. Position a rafter with its upper end snug to the temporary block, and drive nails to attach.

Continued on next page.

Continued from previous page.

11 Set a rafter on the other side of the ridgeboard. Check for tight joints at the ridgeboard and at the wall plates, and drive nails to attach. Remove the blocks.

12 At the bird's-mouth, angle-drive nails into the top plate. Hand-nailing will often split the wood here; use a power-nailer, or drill pilot holes and drive screws.

13 Continue adding rafters. Drive three or four nails through the ridgeboard and into each rafter. Measure to check for correct rafter spacing from time to time.

14 The framing will firm up as you work but will not achieve its real strength until the roof sheathing is installed. Add several more pieces of temporary bracing.

TROUBLESHOOTING RAFTER PROBLEMS

AFTER ALL YOUR CALCULATING, you may find that the rafters don't fit tightly at the wall's top plate or at the ridgeboard. Don't get frustrated; it happens to the best of us. Take the time to make needed adjustments.

Because nobody's perfect, you will probably need to raise or lower the ridgeboard to make the rafter joints nice and tight. Use shims at the bottom to raise the temporary braces, or cut them if needed.

If adjusting the height of the ridgeboard doesn't do the trick, you may need to recut some or all of the rafters.

MOVING A POST

WITH ANY CONSTRUCTION PROJECT, you may encounter unexpected layout problems. Even professional porch builders occasionally find that a post needs to be moved. Doing so is not as difficult as you may think. **(1)** Place a protective scrap board against the post, and whack its bottom with a sledgehammer to free it. You can then simply pull the post away. **(2)** Cut the nails with a grinder equipped with a metal-cutting blade; then sink the nails with a nail set. **(3)** Fill the holes with wood filler; allow to dry; and sand smooth. **(4)** To reinstall the post in a new location, tap it in with a sledge; then attach with angled nails driven into the top and bottom plates.

Rafter Ties and Collar Ties

A rafter tie is a horizontal board, usually a 2-by, that spans horizontally across pairs of rafters near their bottoms. If the ridgeboard is not directly supported by posts, rafter ties are vital structural components; without them, downward pressure on the roof would cause the rafters to splay out, moving the walls outward. Collar ties are similar to rafter ties, but are shorter and are placed near the top of the ceiling. They add some strength, but are not as structurally important as rafter ties and are typically installed only where the ridgeboard is structurally supported. Often collar ties are used ornamentally; for instance, to provide a horizontal surface from which to hang a ceiling fan.

Rafter ties, placed at every other rafter, keep the structure together when there is no strong post supporting the ridge beam.

ADDING RAFTER TIES

project

If your framing requires rafter ties, do not take down the temporary bracing that is holding the rafters up until you have installed the ties. In most cases, the ties are the same-dimensioned lumber as the rafters. Many local codes will require you to install a rafter tie on every other rafter. In most areas, to qualify as a rafter tie, at least part of the board must be attached to the lower third of the rafters.

- Lumber for rafter ties
- Measuring tape
- Pencil
- Framing square
- Circular saw
- Power nailer or hammer with nails
- Drill or impact driver
- Strong screws, as required by code

1 Where a rafter is placed against the house, find studs in the wall of the house, and drive heavy-duty screws through the rafter and into studs. Be sure to use code-approved screws.

2 Use a level to mark the rafters for the lower edge of the rafter ties. The lines should be less than one-third of the way to the top of the framing. Measure along the lines for the length of the ties.

3 To mark for this long, sharp angle, hold a framing square at the same angle as you did for cutting the rafter ends, but make the mark along the other, longer blade of the square.

4 Hold the rafter tie against the marked line, with its top edge flush or nearly flush with the top edge of the rafter. Drive strong screws in a pattern like the one shown to fasten the tie to the rafter along as much of its length as possible.

BUILDING EAVES

YOU COULD LEAVE the rafter ends exposed, but covering them with trim gives them a cleaner and more finished look. And if you are going to add gutters, the fascia provides additional support for them; otherwise, you would be driving gutter spikes into the ends of the rafters. If you will be using wood fascia pieces, it's a good idea to apply at least a coat of primer and, preferably, two coats of paint, before installing them. You can go back and touch up the paint job at the end of the project. Or use vinyl or composite trim boards, which usually do not require finishing.

Because the roof's drip edge and roofing will overhang the fascia board, it is best to install the trim pieces before you sheath the roof with plywood.

1 The piece that attaches to the underside of the eave is called the soffit. Measure and cut it to length; hold it flush with the ends of the rafters; and attach it with three nails driven into each joint.

2 Drive nails to fasten the fascia to the ends of the rafters. Because the rafters may not all be perfectly lined up, site along the fascia to check for straightness. You may need to pry the fascia out at some points; insert a shim; and redrive nails.

3 If the fascia board is not long enough to reach all the way, make a scarf joint, with ends of both boards cut at 45-deg. bevels. This joint can be sanded very smooth.

FRONT OVERHANG FRAMING

A FRONT OVERHANG adds a nice decorative touch, helps keep water away from the front screening, and could provide a bit of shade during the summer. The overhang typically is not as strong as the rest of the rafter framing, but it cannot be simply tacked on; by code, it should be strong enough to support a roof. Here, the ridgeboard was cut to extend past the regular rafters, and the fascia board was also installed byond the edge of the last full-size rafter. Smaller-dimensioned rafters—2x6s rather than 2x8s—attach to the ridgeboard and the fascia for just enough strength.

You could install a straight overhang, but this overhang is at a jaunty angle. The ridgeboard reaches out 16 inches, and the fascia extends only 10 inches. As a result, the overhang rafters angle back toward the porch at their bottoms, as shown in step 3. To accommodate this arrangement, the overhang rafters must be cut with a bevel at both ends. Because these rafters angle at two directions, they need to be cut at a bevel as well as an angle.

1 Measure the distance from the inside of the fascia board to the ridgeboard. With the measuring tape stretched taut, hold an angle square against the tape and the ridgeboard or the fascia board to obtain the bevel at which the rafters will be cut.

2 Mark the rafter with the same angles used for the regular rafters. Set a circular saw to the bevel angle you obtained when you measured, and cut.

3 Position each rafter, and drive nails or screws through the ridgeboard and the fascia to attach.

FRAMING A SHED ROOF

A shed roof often has a shallow slope. This not only lowers its visual profile, but also makes it an easy roof to attach to a house without bumping into a window. On a porch, a shed roof is built something like a deck, with a ledger board that attaches to the house and rafters that attach to the ledger using joist hangers.

Making Shed Rafters

Most of the calculations and cuts for shed rafters are much the same as those for gable rafters; they butt against a ledger at the house rather than a ridgeboard. It's best to install the ledger first; then cut the rafters to fit against it.

You have two basic options: measure and calculate to install the ledger at the correct height for the slope called for in your plan; or install the ledger at a height that makes sense practically and visually, and then hold a board in place and scribe lines for the house cut and the bird's-mouth cut.

Measure and Calculate. Obtain the required roof slope from your plan. To obtain the run, measure from the outside of the wall's cap plate to the house, and subtract the thickness of the ledger. Once you have the slope and the run, use the gauge on a framing square or a framing calculator to determine the rise. (See pages 110–111.) Install a ledger with its top at the top of the rise.

Also calculate to determine rafter length. Add the desired overhang. Mark and cut for the "three crucial cuts," as shown on page 110. Test-fit the rafter; make any needed modifications; and use it as a template for marking the other rafters.

Mark in place. Make rough calculations to be sure your roof slope will be at least as steep as is called for in the plan; then install the ledger. Using a piece of rafter stock longer than it needs to be, make an estimated plumb cut at the upper end. Working with a helper, hold the rafter against the side of the ledger and against the side of the wall; hold the lower portion at the correct height for a bird's-mouth cut. Holding your pencil against the ledger, scribe a line on the rafter for the plumb cut. Also scribe two lines at the wall for the bird's-mouth cut.

You can use a large angle square to mark the plumb cuts, left. It has a gauge that indicates slope ratios.

Finish a bird's-eye cut, below, using a handsaw or saber saw.

SHED ROOF FRAMING BASICS

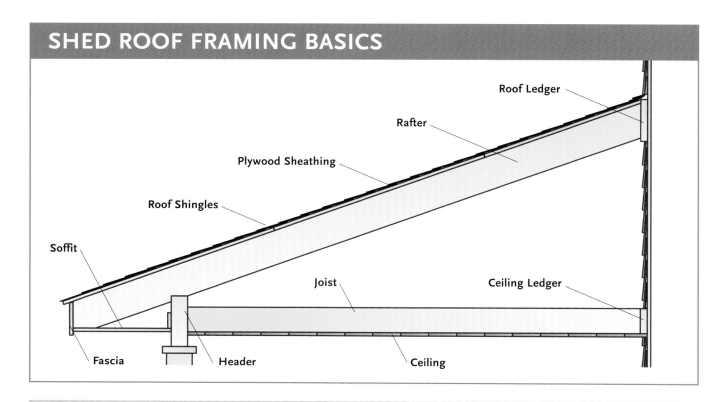

Roof Ledger

Rafter

Plywood Sheathing

Roof Shingles

Soffit

Joist

Ceiling Ledger

Fascia

Header

Ceiling

ATTACHING A LEDGER AND RAFTERS

INSTALL A LEDGER FOR A SHED ROOF much as you would a deck ledger, as shown on pages 86–87. However, you will not need to cut out the siding and install flashing to seal out water; that will be done later when you install roofing.

Unless you are fortunate enough to position the ledger at a rim joist, you'll need to find the wall studs. Use a stud finder, or drive exploratory nails into the siding, where the holes will be covered with the ledger, and mark the wall with the stud locations.

Cut the ledger to fit. In most cases, the ledger is the same length as the wall that is parallel with the house. The roof will overhang it by only an inch or two on each side. Position the ledger at the determined height, and check with a level to be sure its ends are plumb with the ends of the walls that are perpendicular to the house. Be sure the ledger is level, and drive code-approved screws or other fasteners to anchor it firmly to the house.

Joist hangers provide firm attachment points where the roof rafters meet the ledger.

Lay out for the positions of the rafters—usually, on 16- or 24-inch centers on both the ledger and the cap plate. Cut and install rafters as you would on a gable roof, but add joist hangers where they attach at the ledger as you would for deck joists.

Filling in the Triangles

For decorative purposes and perhaps to make screening possible, you can install short posts between the rafters and the tops of the walls that are perpendicular to the house. For symmetry, place these short posts, which really don't serve a structural function, directly above lower posts. That way the eye will follow the line of the post directly up to the rafter line.

Use a level to mark for a post location on the wall's top cap; then use the level to mark for its location on the rafter. Measure between the two lines to determine the post length. Use a framing square to mark the top of the post with the same angle as the roof slope. Cut the post using a power miter saw or a circular saw. Tap the post in place, making sure the post is plumb; and attach by driving angled nails or screws.

Short posts that span between the top of the wall and the roof rafters provide a surface to which you can attach screening.

HURRICANE TIES

MANY BUILDING DEPARTMENTS require hurricane ties, seismic ties, or other special hardware to strengthen roof framing, especially at the joints between rafters and walls. Use the specific pieces that are required. The ties shown below will be hidden when you box in the eaves.

EXTRA-STRONG HURRICANE TIES

A roof with a low slope is more susceptible to getting lifted up by strong winds. Many building inspectors want to see beefy hurricane ties like the ones shown below. Be sure to drive nails into all the holes for maximum strength.

INSTALLING PREFORMED COLUMNS

CYLINDRICAL ARCHITECTURAL COLUMNS are most often used on an open porch; some types of squared columns can be incorporated into a screened porch. Today's columns are made of fiberglass, PVC, composites, fiber-reinforced concrete, and other materials, and they are reasonably priced. Purchase them through a home center or from on-line sources. They can usually be delivered to your home within a week. Have the columns on-site be-fore you build the roof to be sure they will fit.

Most columns are strong enough to be struc-tural—they can support the roof as well as a wood post. However, check with the supplier and your build-ing inspector to be sure that yours will meet local codes. Depending on the type of column, you can build the roof on temporary supports and then install the columns, or install the columns first and build the roof on top of them.

This type of column is made of fiberglass and is held in place using a long threaded rod that inserts down through the middle of the column. Tighten nuts under the decking and on top to hold it in place as you work.

This column is made of fiber-reinforced con-crete. It comes with top and bottom trim pieces that slide into place. The column can be cut to length with a circular saw if needed.

1 Slide the trim pieces onto the column. With the roof sup-ported by temporary posts, raise the column into position.

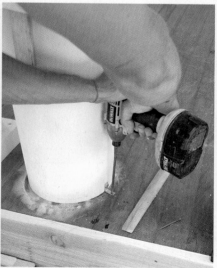

2 Check the column for plumb in both directions. Attach at the bottom and the top with clips and screws.

3 At both the bottom and the top, slide the sleeves into position, and drive finishing nails or screws to attach.

FAUX MASONRY SIDING

COVERING SKIRTING WALLS OR COLUMNS with masonry is not as difficult as you may imagine. Nowadays the most common method is to build walls or columns out of 2x4 framing and pressure-treated plywood, which you then cover with roofing felt and wire mesh. The mesh serves as a base for the mortar. Attach faux stone or brick to the wire mesh by embedding it in mortar.

If you install faux brick, take extra care to keep the units straight and evenly spaced. Carefully fill the joints with mortar as you go, taking care not to smear the bricks. Finish by lightly brushing the surface.

Faux masonry often comes with corner pieces, which wrap around corners to give the impression of a full-thickness of stones or bricks.

1 Cut the pieces using a wet-cutting masonry saw or, as shown here, a grinder equipped with a masonry blade.

2 Mix a batch of mortar that is just barely stiff enough to hold its place. "Back-butter" each piece with plenty of the mortar.

3 Press each piece firmly into the wire mesh. Tap with the handle of your trowel to ensure adhesion.

4 Press squeezed-out mortar back down behind the masonry unit, or smear it against the mesh. Periodically use a level to check for straightness.

roofing 6

ROOFING IS A CONSTRUCTION TRADE unknown to many do-it-yourselfers, so you may choose to hire a professional roofer to install the roofing and flashing, and perhaps the sheathing as well. However, a porch roof is usually pretty straightforward—there are usually no hips, vents, valleys, or complicated flashings around a chimney. So if you've had success with other building projects, you may want to tackle the job yourself. This chapter concentrates on the most common and the simplest methods, using plywood sheathing and composition shingles.

ROOF SHEATHING

If the porch's ceiling will not be covered with a finish material such as bead-board, the underside of the sheathing will show. The simplest solution is to use grooved sheet siding, or T1-11, with the grooves facing down. Another option is to install a finished-looking material such as tongue-and-groove knotty pine.

SHEATHING CLIPS

IF YOUR SHEATHING does not have tongue-and-groove edges, codes require sheathing clips to be installed midway between rafters. After installing the first sheet, slip the clips into place; then guide the next sheet into their grooves. These clips provide rigidity.

smart tip

WHERE SHOULD YOU END?

IN MOST CASES, SHEATHING SHOULD END UP ¾ INCH SHORT OF THE FINISHED EDGE. IF YOU WILL INSTALL FASCIA TRIM LATER, THEN CUT THE SHEATHING FLUSH WITH THE EDGE RAFTER, AS SHOWN IN STEP 5. HOWEVER, IF THERE WILL BE NO FASCIA, CUT THE SHEATHING SO IT COMES ¾ INCH SHY OF THE EDGE AS SHOWN HERE.

project

Here we show installing the most common roof sheathing: plywood, which comes in 4 x 8-foot sheets. Local codes will tell you which thickness of plywood to use, which will depend on your rafter spacing. In most cases, you can use ½-inch plywood, but ¾-inch is a better choice if rafters are spaced 24 inches apart. You may need to attach sheathing clips between the rafters, as shown on the next page.

TOOLS & MATERIALS

- Roof sheathing
- Measuring tape
- Chalk line
- Hammer or nail gun
- Circular saw

3 Working with a saw on a roof can be awkward, so if you need to cut a sheet, it is often easiest to call out the measurements to a helper below and have him or her make the cut. Raise the sheets up through the rafters as you continue to install sheets.

1 The ends of plywood sheets should fall at the center of the rafters. Partially drive nails into the top of the fascia to keep the sheets from sliding off the roof (inset). On each of the end rafters, measure up from the fascia 48 in. Snap a chalk line on the tops of rafters to indicate the top edge of the plywood sheets.

2 Position the first sheet, making sure its inboard edge falls in the center of a rafter and that its top edge is aligned with the chalk line from step 1. Drive two nails at the top; then snap chalk lines over each of the rafter locations to aid in nailing. Drive nails every 6 in. or as required by local codes.

4 Cut the top sheets to size on the ground. Install the plywood at the ridge. Once installed, the sheets meeting at the ridge should come together neatly, with no gaps wider than ¼ in.

5 At the overhang, it is easier to install sheets so that they run long. Then snap a chalk line that is directly above the edge of the rafter below. Adjust a circular saw so that it cuts only through the thickness of the sheathing.

EDGE FLASHING AND UNDERLAYMENT

While some people apply roofing directly onto the plywood sheathing, this is against building codes. Cover your sheathing with underlayment—most commonly, roofing felt—before applying roofing shingles. This will keep the sheathing dry even when condensate forms under the shingles. If ice dams are a problem in your area or if you have a low-pitched roof, it may be best to install ice-guard membrane on at least part of the roof.

smart tip

INSTALL FELT AS YOU ROOF?

IF YOU WILL BE INSTALLING ROOFING SHINGLES IMMEDIATELY, YOU MAY INSTALL ONLY ONE SHEET OF FELT, THEN START INSTALLING SHINGLES. INSTALL ANOTHER SHEET ONCE YOU HAVE REACHED WITHIN A FOOT OF THE TOP OF THE FIRST SHEET.

LAYING ROOFING FELT

project

Installing felt is a simple matter of rolling, stapling, and cutting with a knife. But work carefully because it's important to get the edges precisely positioned, and the felt must lie flat, with no wrinkles or bubbles. Depending on your locale, your inspector may want you to install the drip-edge flashing first, and then install the underlayment on top of the flashing; or you may be told to install the drip edge on top of the underlayment.

TOOLS & MATERIALS

▌ Drip edge flashing ▌ Roofing nails
▌ Tin snips ▌ Utility knife
▌ Roofing felt (30-lb. felt is recommended)
▌ Hammer-type roofing stapler
▌ ¼-inch staples

3 Before laying the felt, clear the area, and pick up all nails. Sweep and/or use a leaf blower to clean away any debris. Unroll a few feet of the felt. Position the edge tightly against the house or the edge of the roof, and begin to unroll. Drive six or seven staples in a tight pattern near the edge (inset) to hold the paper.

4 Continue rolling almost to the end of the sheathing. Check that the bottom edge of the felt is correctly aligned along the flashing—tug on the roll as needed to remove any wrinkles or bubbles.

1 T-shaped drip-edge or drip-cap flashing is the most common type of flashing to apply onto new sheathing. Cut it using a pair of tin snips. To avoid bending the flashing as you cut, make three small cuts rather than trying to cut it all in one snip.

2 Lay the flashing flat on the sheathing so that it covers the edge of the sheathing. Here it is positioned at the corner of the eave and rake edges. Some codes require rake flashing be installed over the roofing felt. Check for requirements in your area. Attach using nails.

5 You can use a standard stapler to attach the felt, but a hammer stapler is much faster. Drive plenty of staples—at least four staples across the width of the felt every 2 ft., or more if it is windy. Cut the felt long; staple the felt down near the edge; then use a utility knife to trim edges cleanly and neatly (inset).

6 Install the next sheet. Use the lines on the felt as guides to overlap the previous sheet by at least 6 in. Install sheets on both sides of the roof if you are building a gable roof; then finish with a sheet that covers the ridge and laps over the sheets on each side.

LAYING ICE GUARD

TO PREVENT DAMAGE FROM ICE DAMS in areas with freezing winters, codes often call for ice guard, also called waterproofing shingle underlayment (WSU). It has a plastic backing that covers the sticky side.

TIP: On a fairly cool day, you can remove the backing and then slide the WSU into place before pressing it onto the sheathing. However, on a hot day the sticky side may be too sticky to slide across the plywood. In that case, slide the WSU into position with the backing still attached. Check that it is correctly aligned; then roll up about half the sheet, taking care not to budge the sheet out of position. Remove the backing as you slowly roll the sheet back onto the sheathing. Gently remove bubbles, but don't press down. Do the same for the other side, and press the WSU onto the sheathing.

1 Measure and cut the WSU to length using a utility knife and a straightedge.

2 Roll the sheet up; then remove the backing plastic as you unroll it. Take care not to wrinkle or bend the WSU as you work, because if two sticky areas touch, they will be difficult to pull apart.

3 Working with a helper, keep the sticky side up while you move it nearly into position. Carefully turn it over; then slide it into correct alignment along the drip-edge flashing. Once you are certain it is correctly aligned all along its length, press down and smooth out any bubbles.

4 If a sheet is not long enough to reach the end, cut another piece long enough so that it overlaps the first sheet by at least 8 in., and install it in the same way.

ROOFING AND FLASHING

Buy composition shingles (which may be primarily asphalt or fiberglass) and flashings as required by local codes. If you are unsure how to install any of the flashings or roofing pieces, it may be best to hire a professional roofer, who can work quickly and guarantee a leak-proof roof.

To install flashings and roofing correctly, it helps to visualize the path of rainwater. Moisture should have no opportunity to seep under any shingles or behind the house's siding. Whenever possible, install shingles and flashings so water runs over them, with no exposed fasteners or tops of flashing. In some cases, however, this will not be possible, and you will need to apply roofing cement to cover an exposed nailhead or the top edge of flashing.

Choose nails of the correct length. They should be long enough to hold firmly, but if the underside of the sheathing will be exposed, they should not poke through. If the porch ceiling will be covered with bead-board or another finish, it's fine to have the nails poke through.

TEST THE PATTERN

LAY SOME SHINGLES on a piece of plywood to test the pattern. You may want to match the pattern on your house's roof. Most shingles have a reveal of 5 inches, meaning you will snap chalk lines 5 inches apart. (See step 3, page 134.) Also decide on the shingle pattern as described below.

CHOOSING A SHINGLE PATTERN

THERE ARE QUITE A FEW possible shingle patterns; here we show the three most popular. The most common method of aligning shingles is called the 6-inch method. Each course starts at a 6-inch offset to the course below. This is handy because it neatly cuts tabs in half and minimizes waste. The result is a neat arrangement where each tab lines up with the tab two courses above and below it.

Though the 6-inch method is the easiest to cut and apply, some builders worry that the neat alignment may create a flow path that could erode shingles. This is a matter of debate, but you may want to choose a pattern that avoids the problem altogether. The 4-inch method is diagonal in appearance with two full shingles between tab slots. The 5-inch method provides a bit more offset and more of a diagonal pattern.

The 6-in. method is the easiest and most common shingling pattern. Alternating tab cutouts are aligned.

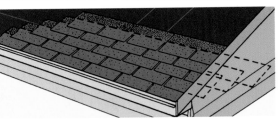

With the 4-in. method, tab cutouts align vertically every fourth course.

A pleasing diagonal effect results when shingles are trimmed in 5-in. increments and tab cutouts never exactly align.

Roofing

LAYING COMPOSITION SHINGLES

project

Roofing is hard work; just getting the shingles up on the roof can be a strain. You could nail shingles by hand, but a pneumatic roofing nailer, which hooks up to a standard compressor, makes the job much easier. It also allows you to concentrate on getting everything straight.

TOOLS & MATERIALS
▌ Measuring tape
▌ Chalk line
▌ Roofing shingles
▌ Roofing nails
▌ Asphalt roofing cement
▌ Hand roofing hammer, standard hammer, or power roofing nailer
▌ Utility knife with extra blades

1 From the bottom and side edges of the underlayment, measure the width of the shingles, and snap chalk lines as shown.

3 At each end, measure up from the bottom of the starter shingles by the determined reveal dimension (most often, 5 in.). Snap a series of chalk lines to indicate the top edges of each course of shingles. Depending on your chosen pattern, gang-cut shingles of various sizes to install at the beginning of each course (inset).

4 Start at one end (called the rake edge) with a shingle that is aligned along the side of the underlayment. Install shingles in a stepped pattern, as shown, using the cut shingles from step 3 in an alternating pattern.

134

2 Install a starter course of shingles along the chalk lines. Some builders prefer to install tab shingles upside down as a starter course. Others use a starter strip made specifically for that purpose; the material comes in rolls.

smart tip

GOOD ROOFING PRACTICES

■ IF A ROOF IS STEEPLY SLOPED, USE ROOF JACKS AND PLANKS TO KEEP FROM SLIDING OFF. MOVE THE JACKS EVERY SIXTH OR SEVENTH COURSE.

■ IF POSSIBLE, SAVE BACK-STRAINING WORK BY PAYING TO HAVE THE SHINGLES DELIVERED ONTO THE ROOF. IF THAT IS NOT POSSIBLE, BE SURE TO INSTALL FIRM SCAFFOLDING OR LADDERS BEFORE YOU START CARRYING SHINGLES UP TO THE ROOF. PLACE A BUNDLE OF SHINGLES ONTO A SHOULDER, AND KEEP YOUR BACK AS STRAIGHT AS POSSIBLE WHILE CARRYING THEM.

■ DO NOT INSTALL ROOFING WHILE THE ROOF IS WET; WAIT FOR IT TO DRY OUT.

■ IF THE WEATHER IS SO HOT THAT YOU INDENT SHINGLES OR DISLODGE GRAINS WHEN YOU STEP ON THEM, STOP WORKING AND START AGAIN ONCE THINGS HAVE COOLED OFF. OTHERWISE YOU MAY DAMAGE THE SHINGLES.

5 Consult the packaging to find the recommended nail pattern for your type of shingle. In most cases, drive 4 or 5 nails per shingle, positioned about ½ in. above the cutout slots or a printed layout line. Drive nails just flush so that they hold the shingle tightly but not so deeply that they dig into the shingle.

6 When you get to the end of a course, measure over for the last piece and cut to fit. Take the time to get a nice straight line, aligned with the underlayment. Some builders prefer to let the shingles run wild past the underlayment. When the shingles are all installed, they strike a chalk line and cut through the shingles all along the line.

Continued on next page.

Roofing

Continued from previous page.

7 Install shingles up to the house; then prepare the house for the flashing, which must slip behind the siding. Siding nails will likely be in the way. In some cases, it's best to remove the siding, install the flashing, then reattach the siding. If possible, pry out some nails and drive others in using a nail set.

8 Slip the flashing up under the siding. Its bottom edge should rest on top of the shingles so that water flows easily from the top of the flashing to the top of the shingles.

9 Cut narrow strips to cover the flashing (inset). You may choose to attach this strip with roofing cement only and no nails. Or drive nails, and then apply dabs of roofing cement to cover the nailheads.

STEP FLASHING

WHERE A GABLE OR HIP ROOF meets the siding at an angle, install bent aluminum step flashing. If possible, it is usually best to remove the siding, install the flashing, then reinstall the siding over the flashing. Attach flashing to walls by driving a nail near the top of each piece. Cover flashing pieces with shingles. Avoid driving nails through the lower part of the flashing.

BENDING FLASHING

SMALL PIECES OF STEP FLASHING can be purchased prebent. However, a long piece of flashing, as with the one needed for where a shed roof meets the house, is best made out of a roll of flat flashing. This gives you one continuous piece.

Use tin snips to cut the flashing to length. Every 2 feet or so along its length, mark the flashing for the place where you will bend it—usually, it should travel 3 inches up under the siding. Tightly clamp a long, straight board along the marks, and check for accuracy. Start bending the flashing by hand, taking care to keep the bend tight to the clamped board and to avoid wrinkles. Then place another board alongside the bent portion, and tap with a hammer to make a nice straight bend.

TOPPING A GABLE OR HIP ROOF

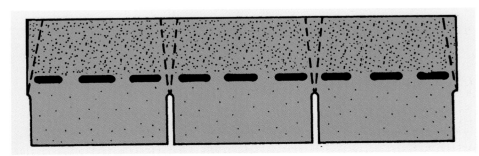

1 Where the roof comes to a peak, cut a series of ridge caps in the pattern shown, with what will be the unexposed ends tapered.

2 Install shingles up along both sides, and trim the last courses so they end at the ridge.

3 Strike a chalk line, and nail the ridge cap shingles so that they overlap evenly on both sides of the ridge. The ridge caps should have the same exposure (usually 5 in.) as the rest of the shingles. You'll end up with a couple of exposed nails; cover them with roofing cement.

137

FILLING BETWEEN ROOFS

It often happens that a porch's roof—especially a gable roof—intersects with the house roof in an awkward way. This can form a pocket where rain and snow will collect and have a difficult time draining away. In most cases, this problem can be solved by building a small section of roofing that ties the house and porch roofs together.

smart tip

CUTTING FRAMING PIECES

CUTTING THE FRAMING FOR THE SMALL SECTION SHOWN HERE IS CHALLENGING. A BIT OF TRIAL AND ERROR MAY BE IN ORDER: CUT PIECES A BIT LONGER THAN NEEDED; THEN HOLD THEM IN PLACE TO MARK FOR MORE ACCURATE ANGLE CUTS. HOWEVER, THEIR EDGES SHOULD FORM A FLAT PLANE FOR SUPPORTING THE PLYWOOD SHEATHING.

A (NEARLY) FLAT ROOF

IF THE DISTANCE to an upper-story window would get in the way of a gable roof and a shed roof is not to your liking, consider a "flat" roof, which is actually slightly sloped—with a pitch of at least ¼ inch per running foot. Because snow will not slide off it easily, you'll need to beef up the framing, using wider and perhaps more closely spaced rafters. A flat roof is probably a job for professional roofers and perhaps professional framers as well.

One common framing method is to frame the roof with rafters that are level; then cut long, sloping "sleeper" pieces that rest on top of the rafters to provide slope.

Flat roofs are not covered with shingles but some type of roll roofing. One common material is modified bitumen, which is applied using a propane torch. The heat from the torch melts the bitumen so that it adheres to the roof deck. This type of roofing is usually applied by a professional.

BUILDING A SMALL FILL-IN ROOF SECTION

project

This sequence shows one example of an awkward intersection of porch and house roof, but your situation will likely look different. Check with your inspector or a roofing contractor to learn the best way to provide smooth drainage, as well as adequate flashing or other protection against water infiltration in case of wind-driven rain. You may, for instance, need to install "valley flashing," which protects the place where two roof slopes meet at the bottom. When in doubt, hire a professional.

TOOLS & MATERIALS

▮ Measuring tape ▮ Chalk line
▮ 2x6 or 2x8 for framing
▮ Plywood roof sheathing
▮ Circular saw ▮ Hammer or nail gun

3 Snap a line marking the outer edge of the new roof section. Once roofing is installed along this line, water can easily run off the roof and into the gutter.

1 In a place like this, rain and snow would collect and almost certainly cause water damage to the porch roof and the house siding.

2 Using the methods shown on pages 112–113, capture the roof's angle, and cut a 2-by ledger to set against the house. Check it for level, and drive nails or screws into studs to attach it.

4 Use an angle square to capture the angle at which you will cut the bottom plate (inset). Cut the bottom plate, and attach it to the roof.

5 Cut rafters as needed. Cut and attach sheathing, flashing, and roofing felt as you did for the main roof. Consult the building inspector for flashing requirements for where they two roof planes meet.

INSTALLING GUTTERS

The instructions here cover installing aluminum components. They show connecting an end cap and a downspout outlet. Use the same methods to attach other aluminum parts. Gutters must slope about 1 inch per every 8 running feet. That means they will be misaligned visually with the roofline, but the slope is necessary so that the water can run freely to the downspout.

TOOLS & MATERIALS

- Measuring tape
- Chalk line ▌ Gutters, downspouts, and fittings
- Tin snips ▌ Gutter caulk
- Drill ▌ Pop-rivet tool
- Saber saw

1 Measure for the length of the gutter sections. Also measure and note the distances to the rafter ends so that you can attach the spikes that are driven into them and not just into the fascia. Snap a chalk line that slopes at least 1 in. per 8 running ft. along the fascia.

5 Equip a saber saw with a metal-cutting blade. In the center of the marked hole, drill a hole large enough for the blade to fit through. Cut the hole.

6 Turn the gutter right side up. Slip the downspout outlet into the hole, and drill four holes, one on each side, through its flange and the gutter. (See step 7.)

GUTTER PARTS

METAL AND VINYL GUTTER HARDWARE includes fittings and fasteners for every situation.

Gutter

Hanger

Downspout

Cap

Bracket

Drop Outlet

Elbows

Connector

Corners

Cap

2 Use tin snips to cut the gutter to length. (If your gutter pieces are not long enough, use a straight connector to attach two pieces.) Slip a cap onto the gutter end; tap it lightly to get it to seat fully.

3 Drill holes for the pop rivets. Insert a pop rivet into the pop-rivet tool (inset). Slip the rivet through each of the holes you drilled, and squeeze the tool to fasten the rivet.

4 Turn the gutter upside down. Where you want a downspout to be connected, hold a downspout outlet in place, and mark for cutting a hole.

7 Fasten with pop rivets from the bottom of the gutter.

8 Apply a generous bead of gutter caulk at all joints, and allow to dry. Try not to touch the caulk with your finger or glove; it's extremely sticky.

9 Drill holes through the front and back of the gutter, positioned so that the spikes will be driven into each of the rafter ends. Hold a ferrule inside the gutter, and slip a spike (here, a screw spike) through the ferrule.

10 Working with a helper, lift the gutter into position, and align it with the chalk line from step 1 so that it is correctly sloped toward the downspout. Drive spikes to attach the gutter.

11 Attach downspouts using elbows and straps, so they attach firmly to a post. At the bottom, attach an elbow, and set a splash block beneath it to direct water away from the house.

finishing the porch 7

BECAUSE A PORCH IS A SIMPLE STRUCTURE, most of the projects in this chapter can be undertaken either after the basic porch is built or while it is under construction. Still, plan carefully to avoid extra work. If the porch floor is low to the ground and difficult to work on from below, for example, it may be best to run some electrical cable before you install the decking. When framing, it may make things easier later if you add extra framing pieces to support the railing or the skirting you will install.

PORCH RAILINGS

For safety, a railing or wall of some sort is usually required on a porch that is 2 feet or more above the ground. Even if your porch is low to the ground, you may want a railing for design purposes and to keep people from bumping into the screening.

Railings are most often installed on the insides of the posts. This keeps them a bit more protected from rain, and well out of the way of the screening. If you will not screen the porch, you may choose to attach the rails to the outside of the posts or run them between the posts.

Check local codes for railing requirements. Codes may call for a railing that is 36 or 42 inches tall. Most codes call for no larger than a 4-inch space between the balusters or between the decking and the bottom of the railing.

BALISTER SPACING

TO EVENLY SPACE BALUSTERS between two posts, measure the distance between the posts, and divide that distance by 5½ inches (4 inches for the allowable space and 1½ inches for the width of a baluster). Round up the result to the next whole number for the number of balusters. Multiply the number of balusters by 1½ inches (the width of a baluster) to get the total amount of width that the balusters will take up. Subtract that number from the distance between the posts to get the total amount of empty spaces. Divide that number by the number of spaces, which is the number of balusters plus one. The result is the ideal spacing between balusters.

For example, if the distance between posts is 68 inches:
- 68 ÷ 5.5 = 12.3; round up to get 13 balusters
- 13 x 1.5 = 19.5 (the total amount of width occupied by balusters)
- 68 − 19.5 = 48.5 (the total amount of width occupied by spaces between balusters)
- 48.5 ÷ 14 (number of balusters plus one) = 3.46
- This means the space between balusters is 3.46 inches, or slightly less than 3½ inches.

BUILDING A BASIC RAILING

project

In the following 12 steps we show installing the most common type of railing, which has 2x4 top and bottom rails, 2x2 balusters (pickets) and a 2x6 top cap. More options are shown on pages 148–149.

TOOLS & MATERIALS

- 2x4s for top and bottom rails
- 2x2s for balusters
- 2x6 or 2x8 for top cap
- 2½-inch deck screws
- Drill ■ Measuring tape
- Power miter saw
- Jigsaw and circular saw
- Router with roundover bit

smart tip

FIGURING RAIL LENGTH

IN THIS DESIGN, THE RAIL ON THE PORCH'S SIDE EXTENDS ACROSS THE FACE OF THE POST, AND THE RAIL ON THE PORCH'S FRONT BUTTS UP TO IT. THAT MEANS THE FRONT RAIL IS CUT 3 INCHES SHORTER THAN THE SPAN BETWEEN THE POSTS (BECAUSE IT IS 1½ INCHES SHORT OF THE POST ON EACH SIDE).

1 Cut the top and bottom rails to length. See the tip opposite bottom to help you figure the lengths of the rails. To give the rail ends a decorative chamfer, mark a square line ¾ in. from each edge of each end and cut at a 45-deg. bevel (inset).

2 Place rails in position against the post, stacked on top of each other. Measure the distance between the posts, and calculate your spacing. Use an angle square to mark the top and bottom rails with the positions of the balusters.

3 Attach a power miter saw to a board, and set up a simple jig like the one shown to cut all the balusters to the same length. It is common practice to cut the bottom ends at a 45-deg. bevel for a light decorative touch.

4 Set the rails in position to test the fit. Use a palm sander to smooth the edges of the balusters and rails and to ease any rough spots.

Continued on next page. **145**

Finishing the Porch

Continued from previous page.

5 Apply stain to all the balusters and rails. This is much easier to do now rather than after the railing is installed, and it will produce neater-looking results.

6 Attach the bottom rails 3½ in. above the decking, and attach the top rails at the finished height of the railing, minus 1½ in. (the thickness of the rail cap). Drive two or three screws into each joint. At a corner, use a square to align the shorter rail.

9 Cut the first 2x6 rail cap to length, and set it in place on top of the top rail. Mark for the sides of each post where you will need to make notch cuts. Use a square to mark for a notch that is 3⅛ in. deep—to cover the top rail and the tops of the balusters.

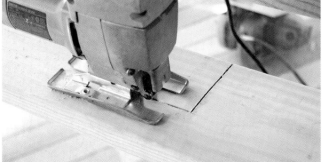

10 Cut as much of the notch as you can using a circular saw; then finish the cut using a saber saw.

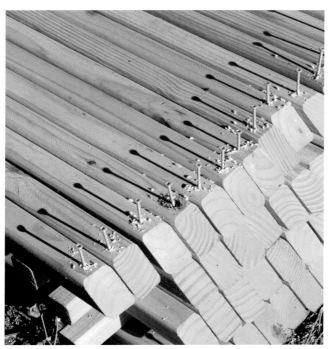

7 To prepare the balusters for installation, drill pilot holes 1¾ in. from each end, and drive screws part-way into the holes.

8 Hold each baluster against the layout line and flush with the top rail, and drive the screw to attach to the top rail. Screw to the bottom rail as well.

11 Test the fit of each cap piece. Equip a router with a roundover bit, and use it to round all the edges, including the insides of the notches.

12 Attach the rail cap with screws. A rounded-over notch fits attractively against a post. A small gap between cap and post is fine; it actually allows water to seep through, thus preventing rot.

Finishing the Porch

OTHER RAILING OPTIONS

RAILINGS CAN BE MADE OF wood, metal, vinyl, composition materials, acrylic or glass panels, cables—or just about any combination thereof. A good number of companies make components for deck railings, and most of them can be used on a porch. Just make sure that balusters and other components will not bump into any screening you will install.

Once you have built the posts or columns, you can order metal railings to fit from a fabricator. They may be made of cast-iron, steel, or aluminum. Install by simply driving one or two lag screws at each joint.

INSTALLING METAL ROD BALUSTERS IN A WOODEN RAILING

1 To install a simple but elegant railing that has metal rod balusters, buy balusters with screw-in connectors. Cut 2x4 or 2x2 top and bottom rails to fit between the posts. Using the calculations from page 144, determine a consistent layout and spacing for the balusters. Lay the rails side by side, and mark for the centers of the balusters. Screw baluster connectors to both.

2 The balusters slip snugly over the connectors. Tap them in place; then attach the entire assembly to the posts.

Don't be afraid to mix components in order to match your style. Here, a vinyl top cap, originally made to be part of an all-vinyl railing system, has been cut to fit and installed over the metal railing.

You can buy components for an old-fashioned railing, with turned balusters and molded top rail. Cut the top and bottom rails, and test the fit. Then, working on a flat surface, attach the balusters by driving screws through the bottoms of the bottom rail. Attach to the top rail using angled trim screws.

Cable railing systems have stainless-steel cables and connectors. They can be installed with metal or wood posts. In this example, the railing is installed outside the posts and screening. Many companies sell do-it-yourself kits. Provide the company with a drawing of your porch, and they will send you all the parts you need. Install the posts and rails, which fit together with a supplied adhesive. String the cables through fittings in the posts, and use the supplied tool and hardware to tighten the cables.

A vinyl or PVC railing system comes in kit form, with posts and balusters cut to fit. Though pricy, they install quickly and need virtually no maintenance. When fitting between porch posts, simply cut the top and bottom rails to fit, and attach with the brackets and screws provided. Depending on the system, you may or may not be able to adjust the spacing between balusters. If you cannot adjust the spacing, you will probably need to have a smaller space between the outside balusters and the posts.

To gain a bit of extra porch space, you can attach the railing to the outside of the posts. Attach 2x4 top and bottom rails that span between the posts. Add a 2x6 or 2x8 top cap; notch it to fit around posts; and have it overhang the top rail by an inch or more in front. Cut 2x2 balusters to fit, and screw them to the back of the rails. You may add second bottom and top rails, which fit between posts, to "sandwich" the balusters.

RUNNING ELECTRICAL CABLE

Most porches have fairly straightforward electrical service: a fan, a couple of light fixtures, and a few receptacles. Usually, all these items will be placed on a single electrical circuit.

Building codes call for underground feed (UF) cable to run from the electrical service panel and under, alongside, or through framing members. In areas with stricter codes, you may be required to run cable through metal or plastic conduit.

These pages show a variety of methods used to route cable through framing members so that only small portions will be visible once the porch is finished. The cable must be protected from nails that will be driven when the trim is installed.

WHO DOES THE WORK?

YOUR BUILDING DEPARTMENT may require all electrical work be done by a licensed electrician. In that case, hire a contractor before you start construction on the porch, and consult with him or her about timing: the contractor will want to run electrical cables at a certain point during construction and install the finish lights, fans, receptacles, and other items near the end of construction. There will probably be two electrical inspections—one for the cables and boxes and one for the finished fixtures and devices. Be sure you do not cover up anything that needs to be inspected.

In some cases, you may be allowed to do much of the grunt work yourself—cutting channels, running cables, attaching boxes, and perhaps installing lights and devices—but the final connection to power at the service panel may need to be done by a licensed electrical contractor. The contractor will be responsible for the whole job, so he or she will supervise and inspect all of your work.

project

RUNNING CABLE FROM BELOW AND UP A POST

Electrical cable is often routed below the porch's deck, either alongside joists or through them. (The process is similar to routing through rafters on page 153.) Consult the building inspector about cutting holes for cables in structural framing. When cutting a path for the cable to emerge above the decking, plan carefully so that all holes will be covered with trim later.

TOOLS & MATERIALS

- UF electrical cable
- Heavy-duty ½-inch drill with a long electrician's bit
- Router with a bit at least ½ inch wide
- Hammer
- Protective nailing plates

smart tip

COVER A LONG GROOVE

A LONG GROOVE PROVIDES PASSAGE FOR ELECTRICAL CABLE TO TRAVEL ALL THE WAY UP THE POST. (A LIGHT-SWITCH BOX IS INSTALLED ON THE OTHER SIDE OF THE POST ABOUT 48 INCHES UP FROM THE FLOOR, AND THE CABLE THEN TRAVELS FROM THE SWITCH UP TO THE CEILING-MOUNTED LIGHTS.) A LONG, CODE-APPROVED METAL PLATE PROTECTS THE CABLE.

1 Equip a heavy-duty drill with a long bit. Near the bottom of the post, drill down and at an angle, as shown, so you avoid drilling through the joists below.

2 Equip a router with a bit wide enough to accommodate one or two cables, and adjust it to cut about ¾ in. deep. Cut a groove up to the location of the electrical box.

3 Run the cable under the deck, and poke it through the hole. Allow at least 8 in. of cable to emerge out the top of the routed groove.

4 Drill a hole near the top of the groove; run the cable through to the inside of the porch; and install a box as shown on the next page. Attach a series of nailing plates to protect the cable. They will be covered by trim later.

Finishing the Porch

Wiring a Ceiling

If the ceiling has exposed rafters, there will be a certain amount of exposed electrical cable as well. However, if it is installed neatly, it will not be very noticeable. A ceiling with finishes that cover the rafters can, as with an indoor ceiling, hide all wiring.

Exposed cable runs alongside a rafter and into a ceiling fan.

This finished ceiling has recessed lights, a fan, and a pendant light. All cables are hidden above the bead-board.

RUNNING CABLE

EVEN A MODEST PORCH will almost always have a ceiling fan with a light. On larger porches, there may be additional lights as well. If the rafters will be covered later with bead-board or another finish, run cable roughly. If the rafters will not be covered, take care to run and staple the cable neatly.

Because it is protected from the elements, indoor-type cable meets most codes for ceiling runs; it is less expensive and easier to work with than the underground feed cable required for exposed locations.

In the example shown here, cable is run through a door opening that will later be framed in, so there was no need to run cable through a groove in the post.

3 For the ceiling fan, use a fan-rated box, which has heavy-duty fastening hardware to firmly hold a fan. (A fan attached to a standard ceiling box may come loose after a year or two of operation.)

UP TO THE CEILING

1 In most cases you will need to drill up through the beam at the top of the wall, which can be demanding physical work. Use a heavy-duty drill, and give the bit a rest to cool down if it starts to smoke.

2 If the rafters will get covered later, you may choose to install recessed canister lights. A "can light" box has arms that quickly attach to rafters on either side. Once attached, the box can slide along the arms for exact positioning.

4 Where cable must run across rafters, drill holes in the centers of the rafters, where nails cannot reach them. If you must drill a hole and install cable within 1½ in. of the bottom of the rafter, install a nailing plate to protect the cable.

5 Where cable runs alongside a rafter, fasten it firmly with cable staples in the center of the rafter's width.

Finishing the Porch

Installing Electrical Boxes

Where wiring will be exposed to the elements, install electrical boxes approved for exterior use. On the ceiling, standard indoor-type boxes are sometimes allowed. In some cases (usually, on a ceiling), it is easiest to install boxes first, then run cable to them; in other cases (usually, on a post), it is easiest to run the cable first.

THE HOME RUN

CABLES ARE RUN FROM THE PORCH to the house's service panel, which is typically located in a basement or garage. The final connection to power is called a home run. Power should be shut off at the main breaker. Cable is run through a knockout hole in the panel and secured with a cable clamp. The cable's sheathing is stripped, and wires are routed around the perimeter of the panel. The neutral (white) wire and the ground (bare or green) wire are connected to the neutral and/or ground bus bar. The hot (black or colored) wire is connected to a new circuit breaker, which is attached to the panel's hot bus bar.

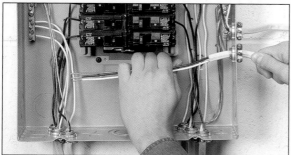

Where cable enters the house, use special fittings to protect the cable, top. The LB fitting shown here is a nipple (short length of threaded pipe) that runs through the house's rim joist. It has plastic bushings to keep cable from rubbing against metal parts. Bottom photo shows how to run new cable into a service panel.

ATTACHING A RECEPTACLE BOX

project

Choose code-approved electrical boxes that are watertight and can receive in-use covers, as shown on page 61. Depending on local codes, you may attach a metal cable clamp, which holds the cable firmly using a setscrew; or you may use a plastic clamp, which grabs the cable without a screw.

TOOLS & MATERIALS

- Electrical box and clamps approved for outdoor use
- Drill
- Lineman's pliers
- Grounding wire connector

3 Grab the bare wire with a pair of pliers, and pull it out of the sheathing. This will also expose the white and black wires.

1 Remove a knockout from the back of the box, and attach a code-approved cable clamp to the hole. Slide the cable or cables through the clamp, and tighten as needed.

2 Press the box into position, and check that it looks straight. Drive screws to attach the box to the post.

4 If you have two ground wires, slip a grounding connector over them. Squeeze with pliers; and twist to join the ground wires together (inset).

5 Cut one of the ground wires near the connector and the other a couple of inches away. Wrap the longer wire around a green grounding screw, and attach the screw firmly to the box. Cut the other wires so that they are about 6 in. long. This box is now ready to receive a receptacle once the rough-in inspection is complete.

Finishing the Porch

SKIRTING

If a porch's deck is raised above the ground more than 16 inches, you will probably want to cover the open space between the deck and the ground. Skirting can be constructed quickly, but it's best to take the time to do it well and get it straight because it will be a noticeable visual element, especially for passersby.

Skirting should be strong enough to withstand bumps. At least parts of it should be removable so that you'll have access to storage space. The area under your porch needs to be well ventilated so that it doesn't become a breeding place for mosquitoes.

HANGING LATTICE SKIRTING PANELS

The most common way to cover the open area under a porch is to build skirting panels made of 2-by lumber and lattice. Attach the panels using screws, or hang them from hooks for easy removal. Use wood lattice—either cedar or pressure-treated—that is a total of ¾ inch thick; thinner panels crack easily.

TOOLS & MATERIALS

▌ Wood or vinyl lattice sheets ▌ 2x2, 2x3, or 2x4 for frames
▌ 2½-inch decking screws ▌ Nails or staples to attach lattice
▌ Hooks and eyes for hanging the panels
▌ Measuring tape ▌ Drill
▌ Level or other straightedge ▌ Circular saw
▌ Hammer or power nailer
▌ Pliers and screwdriver
▌ Wooden stakes (optional)

4 Set a lattice panel on top of the frame. Align two sides of the panel so that they are ¼ in. shy of the edges of the frame boards. You may need to adjust the frame to make it perfectly square so that it aligns correctly. Drive 1½- or 1⅝-in. staples or nails every 6 in. to attach the lattice to the frame.

5 Use a straightedge and pencil to mark for cutting the lattice along the other two sides—again ¼ in. from the outside of the frame. Adjust a circular saw to cut just barely through the thickness of the lattice; then cut along the lines.

1 Measure down from the bottom of the framing to the ground to find the height of the skirting panels. If the ground is not level, remove some of the soil to correct the problem.

2 Lattice panels are only 8 ft. long, so you usually need to use two or more for each side of the deck. Where you will need two panels, mark the center point and measure to there so that the two panels will be the same length.

3 Construct simple frames of 2-by lumber. Make them about 5 in. shorter than the opening to allow 2 in. at the top for the hook and eye and 3 in. of clearance at the bottom. Cut the ends of the boards at 45 deg. Drill two pilot holes and drive screws.

6 About a foot from each end, drill pilot holes up through the bottoms of the outside joist and screw in the hooks (inset). Place the panel in position, and mark for the eyes. Drill pilot holes and drive eyes.

7 Hang the panels on the hardware. You may need to screw or unscrew some eyes or hooks to align the panels symmetrically. In areas with high winds, drive wooden stakes into the ground, and attach the panels to the stakes using screws.

ATTACHING FIXED SKIRTING

IF YOU WILL NOT USE the underside of the porch for storage, build panels and attach them to the posts using screws. You will be able to unscrew them for occasional access. Stain or paint the panels before installing them; once attached, they will be difficult to finish properly.

1 Attach a nailer to the sides of the posts. Position the nailer so that the panel will be flush with the face of the post.

2 Build the lattice panels to fit between the posts. Attach them by drilling pilot holes and driving screws into the nailers.

smart tip

A STRONGER AND NEATER PANEL

TO PRODUCE A CLEANER LOOK, ROUT GROOVES IN 2-BY BOARDS INTO WHICH LATTICE PANELS CAN FIT SNUGLY. CUT THE FRAME PIECES, AND ATTACH TWO OF THEM TOGETHER. CUT THE LATTICE TO FIT INSIDE THE FRAME; SLIDE IT INTO POSITION; AND ATTACH THE OTHER TWO FRAME PIECES.

ACCESS DOORS

AN ACCESS DOOR is not difficult to build. Attach adjacent lattice panels to nailers alongside the posts so that their faces are flush with the post faces. Make a simple frame for the door using 2x3s or 2x4s and lattice. Make the frame ½ in. narrower than the opening to allow for clearance on each side. Attach gate hinges to one side of the door; attach a gate latch to the other side.

SAND AND STAIN

ONCE THE PORCH is basically built, perhaps take a few days off so you can have the energy and patience to do a good, meticulous job sanding, staining, and painting. If the exposed lumber is still damp from the treatment or from weather, give it a few days to dry completely before finishing it.

Exposed lumber—especially pressure-treated lumber—can look much better after a thorough sanding to remove stains and at least some of the printing. Sanding allows the stain to penetrate more deeply. Wear a dust mask when sanding pressure-treated lumber.

Experiment with sanding and staining scrap pieces to achieve the final look you want. Wait a day for the stain to dry and achieve its final appearance.

1 A high-quality palm sander that vibrates as it rotates will remove stains without creating sanding lines. Use 80- or 100-grit sanding disks, and change them when they wear out.

2 Move the sander evenly along the entire surface of boards, exerting only moderate pressure. Where you encounter a stain, allow the sander to linger until the stain disappears or lightens to your satisfaction.

3 Thoroughly mix the stain. To apply stain evenly over large surfaces, use a 5-gallon bucket, a mesh bucket grid, and a narrow roller.

4 Use a brush to stain narrow surfaces. Avoid overwetting the brush, which can lead to drips. Wherever possible, finish with a long, sweeping brush stroke.

SCREENING

If you want screen panels that can be removed for cleaning or repair, check out online sources and local fabricators; the various types are discussed on pages 42–43. Here we show the simplest method—stapling screening onto the posts; then covering the staples with trim.

Some would object that this method makes removal and repair difficult. But if you use very strong screening, sometimes called by names like "super screening," you literally may never need to replace it. And if you do need to replace the screening, it's really not difficult to pry out the trim, pull out the staples, and reinstall.

INSTALLING SCREENING

project

Buy rolls of screening that are wide enough to span across the posts. You will probably end up wasting a good deal of screen material. Don't try to staple with a standard hand stapler. Instead buy or rent a pneumatic wide-crown stapler, and use staples that are 1½ inches wide.

TOOLS & MATERIALS

▐ Extra-strong screening material
▐ Measuring tape
▐ Utility knife
▐ Pneumatic wide-crown stapler
▐ Wide-crown staples at least ⁵⁄₁₆ inch long
▐ Trim boards

4 If you see any waves in the screen, remove one staple; pull taut; and restaple. Drive staples at angles as shown, every 2 to 3 in. Start at the top; then staple the bottom. Pull the screening slightly taut as you work; don't overpull, because you may create waves.

5 Staple the sides next. Start with a staple about one-third of the way down; then drive one about two-thirds of the way down; then fill in the middle with staples every 2 to 3 in. Again, pull slightly on the screen, and take care not to create waves.

1 Measure the height of the opening. Add 4 in. so that there is an extra 2 in. at the top and at the bottom.

2 Roll out the screening on a clean, flat surface. Measure and mark for the cut at the top and bottom of the screening. Slip a straight board under the screening, aligned with the cut marks, and use it as a guide as you cut the screen using a utility knife.

3 Drive a staple at the upper left corner; then stretch the screening fairly tight, and drive a staple at the upper right corner. Pull straight down and slightly to the left, and drive a staple into the lower left corner. Then staple the lower right corner.

6 On the side where the screening runs long, cut it about 1 in. beyond the staples. Install the next screen section in the same way.

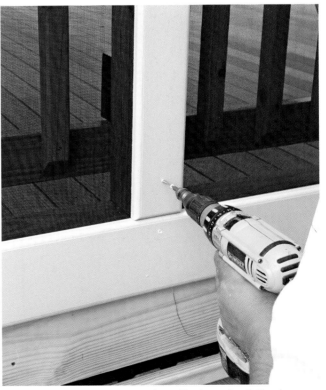

7 Install trim pieces, as described on the following pages, to cover the staples.

FINISHING WITH TRIM

Trim boards largely make up the public face of your porch. You could simply cut pieces to fit, using 1x4s to cover the posts and wider boards for the horizontals. But you'll thank yourself years later if you take the time to use a router to create edge details as shown here. Or use pieces of cove or other decorative trim molding in combination with 1-by boards to create a custom look.

PREPARING TRIM

MEASURE AND CUT the trim boards. Hold them in position where they will go to be sure they fit; then mark reference numbers on their backs so you know where they will go.

Equip a router with a roundover bit, and use it to create a finished edge along all the edges, as well as at the ends (top left and right). Apply primer, then two coats of exterior paint, to all edges that will be exposed (bottom).

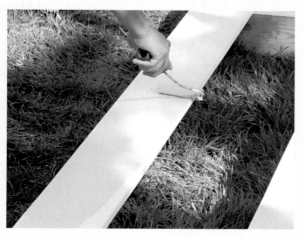

SCALLOPED UPPER TRIM

GRACEFUL SCALLOPS that arch above each of a porch's openings create a classic look. In this example, another piece of trim is added above the scalloped piece for a more textured look.

1 Measure across the front and the sides of the porch at the top of the porch wall. Cut pieces at 45-deg. bevels, so you will have mitered corners.

4 Use a saber saw to cut along the curved line (inset). If other openings are the same size, you can use the cutout as a template for cutting them.

2 Temporarily attach the trim boards. Check for tightly mitered corners, and make adjustments as needed. From the inside, scribe the back of the boards to indicate the openings between the posts. Remove the boards.

3 Place a board scribed side up. Measure and mark the center of the opening. Temporarily attach a perpendicular board to the trim board at the center mark. Make a compass using a string, screw, and pencil. Experiment with different string lengths until you are satisfied with the curve.

5 Use a belt sander to smooth the curved line; then use a router with a roundover bit to finish the edge (inset). Sand away any burrs, and apply paint and primer.

6 Reattach the trim boards. Install an upper piece to finish the look.

porches 8
with pizzazz

FOR MUCH OF THIS BOOK, we've shown building the basic bones of

a porch. This chapter presents projects with additional flourishes and

amenities, some of which you may choose to add to your porch. Profes-

sional porch builders constructed these projects, but competent do-it-

yourselfers with good carpentry skills, patience, and time can achieve

many of the extras you see here. A modern fireplace, for example, comes

as a unit that you just install inside standard framing and then cover with

faux stone. And a spa is typically set onto framing that in turn rests on

concrete footings much like those used to support a deck.

FOUR-SEASON PORCH WITH A DECK ABOVE

The simple lines of this porch were carefully planned for symmetry, making it a graceful classic. In an area with mild winters, people can enjoy porch living year-round. The porch supports a second-level tiled deck that is open to the world.

The porch is supported with a continuous concrete footing (rather than individual footings), which is covered with natural-looking faux brick. Ventilation openings in the foundation are covered with grates to keep out critters. The framing consists of 6x6 posts at the corners with regularly spaced 4x4 posts between them. Above the porch, a drainage system ensures that all water from the upper deck drains into gutters. All exterior surfaces are clad with PVC.

Torch-down roofing —roofers use propane torches to melt the asphalt-backing on the material—covers the porch's nearly flat roof. Treated plywood and cement backer board form the solid substrate for the tile deck floor.

The house wall is covered with the same narrow beadboard as the material used on the ceiling. The flooring, as well as some of the trim and the fireplace mantle, is made of darker-colored tongue-and-groove ipé. Pure white trim, electrical cover plates, windows, and furniture crisply contrast with the natural wood.

A corner gas-powered fireplace adds a homey touch as well as a source of heat. Although it looks like a masonry fireplace, it is really a metal firebox encased in wood framing and covered with backer board and faux stone. It has a raised stone hearth so you can sit right by the fire. The mantle was custom made of ipé lumber.

In a warm climate, wall-mounted heating units, left, and well-insulated doors and windows make the porch livable on all but the coldest nights. Heating units like these require a separate electrical circuit. The porch's ceiling and floor are insulated.

Short knee walls, below, provide a base for acrylic window systems. The windows are in four sections. Three sections slide all the way up to capture maximum breezes in the summer; when closed, they offer protection from the elements.

167

Porches with Pizzazz

RAISED PORCH WITH A CABIN FEEL

From the outside, this second-story porch blends perfectly with the contemporary design of the house and the suburban setting. From the inside, it feels like a rustic retreat.

This porch is built at the second story, providing space for a shady patio below. Scalloped trim joins together the evenly spaced posts at their tops, creating a playful rhythm. An open upper deck is located just off the porch, making the space even more flexible.

A few old-fashioned touches, left, give the interior country charm. Three-foot-high knee walls make the room seem more like a cabin than a modern porch. The short windows above the main windows are reminiscent of old-fashioned transoms, and lantern-style sconce lights add a rustic touch.

The screened windows were fabricated after the framing and fastened with a few screws so that they can be removed easily. The perpendicular strip on the ceiling subtly divides the porch into two equal sections, one for dining and one for sitting and lounging. The fireplace is in the center of the lounging section.

Pine bead-board covers the ceiling of the porch. Variations in color and grain, as well as occasional knots, make it lively yet soothing. To achieve a light color, the bead-board was sealed but not stained. Recessed canister lights provide illumination without calling attention to themselves; ceiling fans make a more decorative statement.

Ample space, above, is provided for a dining table that seats six. The knee walls hide diners from the view of passersby but allow for an expansive view. The ceramic tiles have the look of natural stone, with slight variations in color, which makes for a smooth and easy-to-clean surface while complementing a cabin style. Installing tile on a second-story floor calls for extra-strong framing and sheathing.

Black aluminum screen sections add clean defining lines to the windows. The knee walls are built with stud framing and covered with PVC, which is easy to wipe clean, never needs painting, and will not rot.

Faux stone, left, covers a fireplace positioned so that furniture can be symmetrically arranged on either side.

A SEPARATE SPACE

This second-story porch and deck have the best of the old and the new, combining modern-looking architectural lines with knotty woodwork. The porch flows seamlessly onto the open deck.

Most porches are essentially adjuncts to the house, with a roof and at least one wall that tie into the house. Here the porch is essentially its own structure, with a roof that doesn't attach to the house at all. In addition to adding interesting architectural lines, this allows for a high, vaulted ceiling. Though built high, construction is in many ways conventional, with 6x6 posts atop footings. In this casual setting, the owners felt comfortable leaving the posts exposed rather than cladding them with trim.

Porches with Pizzazz

The upper portion of the porch is clad in wide tongue-and-groove cedar. The trimwork is straightforward, using 1-by lumber rather than molding pieces. Because the woodwork is so exposed, attention to detail is important. Lumber must be dry and of high quality so that it will not warp, crack, or shrink. Cut pieces should meet perfectly flush with other pieces. And though it has a natural look, the wood must be kept well sealed. A good sealer will not only keep out the rain but will also provide UV protection, which prevents the sun from turning the boards gray. In many areas, sealing will be a yearly maintenance procedure.

Though the porch is essentially completely open to the world, knotty paneling and dark furniture pieces make it feel warm and cozy.

The porch and deck, above, were built at the same time. The deck runs alongside the house at a width of about 8 feet, allowing for occasional furniture pieces and wide traffic lanes. The decking runs seamlessly from the deck into the porch. Screening reaches all the way to the floor, with no knee wall. The screen panels are made with simple metal frames. Extra-strong screen material is used; it will not tear or sag even if it gets bumped. Its charcoal color and tight weave render the inside of the porch dark when viewed from outside but barely inhibit the view from inside (inset).

The composite decking has the look and even texture of natural wood but none of the maintenance problems. Because it is not tongue-and-groove and has gaps between the decking boards, screening protects the area under the porch so that mosquitoes and other bugs cannot get in.

OPEN PORCH WITH FIREPLACE AND SPA

From the outside, this porch blends almost imperceptibly with the house and does not call attention to itself. But inside it packs a lot of wow, with its slate floor, cedar ceiling, fireplace, and built-in spa.

This porch's low-pitched shed roof contrasts with the house's roofline, but because it is only 14 feet long and is fairly flat and high, it is barely visible. It's covered with metal roofing—which is a bit pricy but sheds water and lasts for many decades. Posts and beams are made of pressure-treated lumber that is wrapped with PVC fascia material and trim pieces. The siding is fiber-cement board, which looks like beveled wood siding but is less expensive and more durable.

The spa does not actually rest on the floor but is supported by underlying framing that rests on four large concrete footings. To support the tiles, the floor must be very firm. This one is built with 2x10 joists on 12-in. centers, supported by posts and extra-large footings. The joists are covered with ¾-in. treated plywood, topped with cement board. Slate tiles are mortared onto the cement board.

Stained cedar above and the natural slate tile below create a space that feels just the right size—cozy and embracing but not at all cramped. The ceiling is made of 2x6 tongue-and-groove cedar. Because of its thickness and strength, it also acts as the roof sheathing; no plywood sheathing is needed. It is strong enough to span the 32-in. distance between the beams. Before designing a ceiling/roof like this, consult with local codes to learn requirements for rafters and spans.

The modern fireplace is a metal unit light enough to be installed on top of floor framing, without additional concrete footings. It is surrounded by a lumber and plywood box that is covered with faux stone, which can be simply mortared in place. The mantle is installed using brackets that tie it into the framing; the stones cover the brackets. The raised hearth is also built of lumber, plywood, and faux stone.

OPEN PORCH-AND-DECK COMBO

A high vaulted ceiling and open framing allow porch space and deck space to flow seamlessly. Though the porch is built carefully with impressively clean lines, a variety of informal materials and colors lend a happy casual feel.

This porch is essentially a roof built atop a raised deck, though the framing below must directly support the posts that hold up the roof. In particular, the center post, which supports the ridge beam, must rest atop a lower structural post that in turn is supported by a solid footing. The railing here is really part of the deck, not the porch. Posts are made of 6x6s, which are then widened using 2-by lumber and wrapped with PVC trim for a massive look.

The ceiling consists of beautiful smooth cedar. The framing is a 4x12 ridge beam and 4x6 rafters spaced 3 ft. apart. The roof's sheathing is 2x6 tongue-and-groove cedar planks; the bottom of the planks are exposed to make a wonderfully rustic ceiling. Rafters can be spaced this far apart only if the roof's sheathing is strong enough. Wiring for the fan runs up through the posts and through conduit across the top of the ridge beam. Because the posts are built out to make them larger, there is plenty of space to run the cable for the sconces between the PVC trim and the post.

Simple PVC decking carries through the deck into the porch. It is not an interesting-looking material, but it does provide a nice neutral backdrop for carpeting and furniture, and it is very easy to maintain.

ENTRY PORCH DELUXE

A wide entry porch with Greek-style columns and multilayered trim on the roof fascia spruces up the house and provides a neighbor-friendly space for visiting and lounging.

This porch doesn't just blend with the house's architecture; it adds plenty of visual pop. An extra-wide band of multipieced trim runs along the top, enlivened and accentuated by the bump-out in the middle. The location of upper-story windows made it necessary to install a nearly flat roof here. Pure white trim, columns, and stair risers are definitely in the colonial style, although they are made with modern PVC materials. Though it is modest in size, this entry porch has elaborate details that call for very good carpentry skills. You'll need to hire an architect to make detailed drawings. Layered trim like this calls not only for a good deal of trimwork but for precisely installed underlying framing as well.

Faux brick cladding covers the continuous concrete foundation; it complements pristine-white vinyl trim used on the edge of the floor and the stairs.

Unfinished ipé flooring achieves a look that is both sophisticated and casual.

PORCH WITH DEEP WOOD TONES AND DECORATIVE RAFTERS

This porch features lots of natural wood, most of it dark-toned ipé. It may look modest from the outside, but a vaulted ceiling with partially exposed rafters and above-the-beam windows in the front add plenty of drama to the interior.

The porch's design and basic framing plan is straight-forward. But the meticulously installed materials—hardwood posts, rafters, and trim—give it a rich look. It contrasts strongly with the painted siding of the house. Such a difference in styles would look awkward on the front of a house but can be a welcome change of pace in the backyard.

Even the electrical receptacles are trimmed with ipé, left. Here a piece of decking is modified to make a coverplate.

Aluminum screen panels, right, were made by a local fabricator and are sandwiched between two pieces of 1x2 ipé. The ipé can be easily removed by taking out the screws.

The house's siding is covered with the same hem-fir bead-board used on the ceiling of the porch. The rafters are made of 2x10 ipé—which is expensive but adds a unique touch. After framing, the builder installed rafter ties, taking care to keep them level and at the same height. Then he installed bead-board to the ceiling, attaching it to the rafter ties to form the flat portion of the ceiling. As a result, the rafters seem to disappear into the ceiling.

OPEN BACK PORCH WITH GENTLY ARCHED CEILING

The crisp, simple lines of this unscreened porch gently decorate an otherwise plain back façade. Most materials are easy-to-maintain PVC and composite decking. From the inside, an eye-catching long ceiling, covered with natural-wood bead-board, appears to be curved.

The roof has a low 3-in-12 slope, so WSU (waterproofing shingle underlayment), rather than roofing felt, covers the roof sheathing. Standard composite shingles top the porch. In some locales you may be required to install roll roofing or metal roofing for such a low-sloped roof. Unlike the roof, the yard slopes dramatically, so on one side the deck is near grade while the other side is 7 ft. above grade.

The posts are made from 6x6s and clad with PVC boards, then wrapped with simple base trim at the bottoms. To make for a spacious, wide-open feel, posts are spaced widely apart so that the beams span about 12 ft. at the sides and 16 ft. at the front. To carry the load, the beams are LVL (laminated veneer lumber) rather than standard 2-bys. In addition to being strong, the beams are perfectly straight, which adds to the porch's pristine appearance. The railing is a kit that combines PVC posts and rails with metal balusters.

The deck is lowered two steps down from the house's floor so that the porch railing does not block the view from inside the house.

The porch is spacious enough to allow for four ample seating or dining areas. The decking is a composite material whose color coordinates with the natural wood tones of the ceiling.

The ceiling, left, is covered with tongue-and-groove hem-fir, and the middle beam is clad with cedar. The ceiling/roof is framed with rafter ties whose bottoms are about two-thirds of the way to the ceiling. Because of the low pitch of the roof, the effect is to make the ceiling look curved. Both the hem-fir and the cedar are clear, with no knots. Clear lumber is expensive, but knotty wood would have looked out of place. The hem-fir is a material made for interior rather than exterior applications, so it must be covered with two good coats of polyurethane sealer. If wood like this is exposed to direct sunlight, the sealer should have some pigment to protect against UV rays.

Resource Guide

This list of manufacturers and associations is meant to be a general guide to additional industry and product-related sources. It is not intended as a listing of products and manufacturers represented by the photographs in this book.

MANUFACTURERS

Andersen Windows
100 Fourth Ave. N.
Bayport, MN 55003
800-426-4261
www.andersenwindows.com
Manufactures windows and doors.

Buena Vista Sunrooms
8274 Quincy St.
Ventura, CA 93004
800-747-3324
www.sunroom.com
Builds sunrooms, greenhouses, skylights, and other glass structures.

Casablanca Fan Co.
7130 Goodlett Farms Pkwy., Ste. 400
Memphis, TN 38016
888-227-2178
www.casablancafanco.com
Manufactures outdoor ceiling fans.

CertainTeed
P.O. Box 860
Valley Forge, PA 19482
800-233-8990
www.certainteed.com
Manufactures exterior and interior building products.

Chadsworth Inc.
277 N. Front St.
Historic Wilmington, NC 28401
800-265-8667
www.columns.com
Manufactures wood, fiberglass, polyester composite, and PVC columns.

ChoiceDek
Weyerhaeuser NR Co.
800-951-5117
www.choicedek.com
Manufactures composite decking made with recycled materials.

Colebrook Conservatories
152 Stillman Hill Rd.
Winsted, CT 06098
800-356-2749
www.colebrookconservatories.com
Designs, builds, and installs glass enclosures and structures.

Colonial Columns
2102 Pasket Lane
Houston, TX 77092
877-681-2583
www.colonialcolumns.com
Creates custom columns out of various materials.

Daltile Corp.
7834 C.F. Hawn Fwy.
Dallas, TX 75217
214-398-1411
www.daltileproducts.com
Produces exterior tile, natural stone tile, and slabs.

Energy Star
1200 Pennsylvania Ave. NW
Washington, DC 20460
888-782-7937
www.energystar.gov
Provides information on energy-efficient products and home-improvement ideas.

EverGrain
P.O. Box 1404
Joplin, MO 64802
800-253-1401
www.evergrain.com
Manufactures durable compression molding decking materials.

Fiberon
181 Random Dr.
New London, NC 28127
800-573-8841
www.fiberondecking.com
Manufactures fade- and stain-resistant composite decking and railing.

Four Seasons Sunrooms
5005 Veterans Memorial Hwy.
Holbrook, NY 11741
800-368-7732
www.fourseasonssunrooms.com
Designs, builds, and sells sunrooms, solariums, and patio enclosures.

Fypon, Ltd.
960 W. Barre Rd.
Archbold, OH 43502
800-446-3040
www.fypon.com
Manufactures exterior trimwork, including columns and column-cladding systems.

Geodeck
1518 S. Broadway
Green Bay, WI 54304
877-804-0137
www.geodeck.com
Manufactures composite decking materials.

Gerkin Windows & Doors
P.O. Box 3203
Sioux City, IA 51102
800-475-5061
www.gerkin.com
Manufactures energy-saving window and door products.

GRK Fasteners
1499 Rosslyn Rd.
Thunder Bay, ON P7E 6W1
Canada
800-263-0463
www.grkfasteners.com
Offers a line of coated screws and fasteners for different applications.

Hampton Conservatories
288 Broadway
Huntington, NY 11746
877-884-8500
www.hamptonconservatories.com
Designs custom conservatories and solariums.

JELD-WEN, Inc.
P.O. Box 1329
Klamath Falls, OR 97601
800-535-3936
www.jeld-wen.com
Manufactures windows and doors for interiors, exteriors, and patios.

Jim Waters Corp.
419 Manchester Rd.
Poughkeepsie, NY 12603
845-452-6300
www.jimwaters.com
A wholesale distributor of exterior building products.

Marston & Langinger
212-575-0554
www.marston-and-langinger.com
Designs and builds custom-made glass buildings.

Marvin Windows and Doors
P.O. Box 100
Warroad, MN 56763
888-537-7828
www.marvin.com
Manufactures various styles of windows and doors.

Master Window Systems, Inc.
2060 DeFoor Hills Rd.
Atlanta, GA 30318
404-355-5844
www.masterwindowsystems.com
Manufactures vinyl window products.

Maxxon Corp.
920 Hamel Rd.
P.O. Box 253
Hamel, MN 55340
800-356-7887
www.maxxon.com
Provides flooring underlayment products for new construction, remodeling, and renovation.

Melton Classics, Inc.
P.O. Box 465020
Lawrenceville, GA 30042
800-963-3060
www.meltonclassics.com
Manufactures architectural columns, balustrade systems, moldings, and architectural details.

Patio Enclosures
800-230-8301
www.patioenclosures.com
Offers custom sunrooms, solariums, and screen enclosures.

Pella Windows & Doors
102 Main St.
Pella, IA 50219
641-621-1000
www.pella.com
Builds energy-efficient windows and doors.

PGT Industries
800-282-6019
www.pgtindustries.com
Manufactures impact-resistant windows and doors.

Resource Guide

Pilkington Glass Co.
811 Madison Ave.
Toledo, OH 43604
800-221-0444
www.pilkington.com
Manufactures glass building products, including self-cleaning glass.

PorterCorp.
4240 N. 136th Ave.
Holland, MI 49424
616-738-0995
www.portersips.com
Manufactures factory-engineered building products for exteriors.

PPG Industries
1 PPG Pl.
Pittsburgh, PA 15272
412-434-3131
www.ppg.com
Manufactures glass, paints and coatings, and specialty materials.

PVC Industries
107 Pierce Rd.
Clifton Park, NY 12065
518-877-8670
www.pvcindustries.com
Manufactures vinyl windows and patio doors.

Renaissance Conservatories
132 Ashmore Dr.
Leola, PA 17540
800-882-4657
www.renaissanceconservatories.com
Designs, manufactures, and builds glass conservatories.

Screen Tight
1 Better Way
Georgetown, SC 29440
800-768-7325
www.screentight.com
Manufactures home improvement products such as screening, and wood and vinyl screen doors.

Senco Products, Inc.
4270 Ivy Pointe Blvd.
Cincinnati, OH 45245
800-543-4596
www.senco.com
Manufacturer of air-powered fastening tools.

Shadoe Track
London, ON
Canada
800-742-3632
www.shadoetrack.com
Manufactures deck fastening systems.

Tanglewood Conservatories, Ltd.
15 Engerman Ave.
Denton, MD 21629
800-229-2925
www.tanglewoodconservatories.com
Creates custom conservatories, greenhouses, and pool and spa enclusres.

TEMO Sunrooms
20400 Hall Rd.
Clinton Township, MI 48038
800-344-8366
www.temosunrooms.com
Manufactures sunrooms, including thermal sunrooms.

Tiger Claw
400 Middle St., Suite J
Bristol, CT 06010
800-873-2529
www.deckfastener.com
Manufactures hidden deck fasteners.

TimberTech
894 Prairie Ave.
Wilmington, OH 45177
800-307-7780
www.timbertech.com
Manufactures decking, railing, lighting, and fencing materials.

Timeless Architectural Reproductions, Inc.
2655 Northgate Ave.
Cumming, GA 30041
800-665-4341
www.timelessarchitectural.com
Designs and manufactures classic architectural products.

Trex
800-289-8739
www.trex.com
Manufactures wood-alternative decking and railing products.

Trim-Tex
3700 W. Pratt Ave.
Lincolnwood, IL 60712
800-874-2333
www.trimtexinc.com

Manufactures and distributes vinyl drywall beads and drywall finishing accessories.

Tri-State Wholesale Building Supplies
1550 Central Ave.
Cincinnati, OH 45214
888-381-1231
www.tri-statewholesale.com
Manufactures and distributes building materials for remodeling and new construction.

Veranda
2801 E. Beltline N.E.
Grand Rapids, MI 49525
877-463-8379
www.verandadeck.com
Manufactures composite decking and railing.

Werner Co.
93 Werner Rd.
Greenville, PA 16125
888-523-3371
www.wernerladder.com
Supplies aluminum, wood, and fiberglass ladders, step stools, and ladder accessories, such as planks and platforms.

Westview Products
1350 S.E. Shelton St.
Dallas, OR 97338
800-203-7557
www.westviewproducts.com
Designs sunrooms.

Wolmanized Wood
Arch Wood Protection, Inc.
5660 New Northside Dr., Ste. 1100
Atlanta, GA 30328
678-627-2000
www.wolmanizedwood.com
Manufactures various forms of treated lumber for diverse projects.

ASSOCIATIONS

APA—The Engineered Wood Association
7011 S. 19th St.
Tacoma, WA 98466
253-565-6600
www.apawood.org
APA is a nonprofit trade association that works to promote the growth of the engineered wood industry.

AWCI—The Association of the Wall and Ceiling Industries International
513 West Broad St., Suite 210
Falls Church, VA 22046
703-538-1600
www.awci.org
Provides information on wall and ceiling systems, including exterior insulated panels.

International Code Council
500 New Jersey Avenue, N.W., 6th Fl.
Washington, DC 20001
1-888-422-7233
www.iccsafe.org
The International Code Council provides the construction codes and standards that are used on job sites throughout the country.

NAHB—National Association of Home Builders
1201 15th St., NW
Washington, DC 20005
800-368-5242
www.nahb.org
Trade association that helps promote the policies that make housing a national priority.

Southern Forest Products Association
2900 Indiana Ave.
Kenner, LA 70065
504-443-4464
www.sfpa.org
SFPA works to develop and expand market opportunities for Southern Pine forest products. Visit the Web site for industry statistics or to sign up for their weekly newsletter.

Structural Insulated Panel Association
P.O. Box 1699
Gig Harbor, WA 98335
253-858-7472
www.sips.org
A non-profit trade association committed to providing quality structural insulated panels to the construction industry.

Timber Framers Guild
P.O. Box 295
9 Mechanic St.
Alstead, NH 03602
559-834-8453
www.tfguild.org
The organization is dedicated to establishing training programs for timber framers, disseminating information about timber framing, and generally promoting the craft.

Glossary

Actual dimension (lumber) The exact cross-sectional measurements of a piece of lumber after it has been cut, surfaced, and dried.

Actual length (rafters) Length of a rafter after half the thickness of the ridgeboard has been subtracted.

Air-dried lumber Wood seasoned by exposure to the air without use of artificial heat.

Allowable span Distance allowed between two contact points for load-supporting lumber such as rafters, girders, beams, and joists.

Anchor bolt Bolt set in concrete or held in place by friction or epoxy that is used to fasten lumber, columns, girders, brackets, or hangers to concrete or masonry walls.

Angle iron Structural steel bent at 90 degrees and used for fastening a range of framing connections.

Asphalt shingle Shingles made of felt that has been soaked in asphalt; asphalt shingle tabs are coated with granular minerals.

Attic The space between the rafters and the ceiling joists.

Backfill Soil or gravel used to fill in between a finished foundation and the ground excavated around it.

Backing (hip rafter) Bevel cut along the crown edge of a hip rafter that allows plywood from opposing roofs to meet at a clean angle flush with the rafter.

Barge rafters The last outside rafters of a structure. They are usually nailed to outriggers and form the gable-end overhangs. Sometimes called flying rafters.

Batt insulation A mineral fiber material, delivered in rolls and typically paper- or foil-faced, which is installed in stud bays to provide insulation.

Batten Narrow 1-by or 2-by wood strips that typically cover vertical joints between siding boards in board-and-batten siding.

Batter board A level board attached to stakes and used to position string in foundation and footing outlines. Notches in batter boards determine the position of foundation guideline strings.

Bay window A window, typically three sided, which projects from a wall, creating a recessed area in the structure's interior. Also called an oriel.

Beam A steel or wood member installed horizontally to support some aspect of a structure's load.

Beam hanger A metal pocket- or shelf-like hanger that supports a beam where it butts into another member.

Bevel An angled surface not at 90 degrees, typically cut into the edge of a piece of lumber. Also a tool for making such an angle.

Bird's mouth The notch cut near the tail end of a rafter where it fits on a cap plate or horizontal framing member.

Blocking 1) Horizontal blocks inserted between studs every 10 vertical feet to defeat the spread of fire. 2) Lumber added between studs, joists, rafters, or other members to provide a nailing surface for sheathing or other material.

Board-and-batten siding A siding style that uses long siding boards installed vertically, right next to one another, with the gaps between them covered by 1-by or 2-by battens.

Board foot Unit of volume for a piece of wood 12 inches square and 1 inch thick.

Bottom plate The horizontal plate at the base of a wall.

Bridging Wood blocks installed in an X-shape between floor joists to stabilize and position the joists.

Built-up beam or girder A beam or girder made of smaller component parts—for example, nailing together three 2x12s for a "built-up" beam.

Butt joint The junction where the ends of two pieces of lumber or other members meet in a square-cut joint.

Cantilever Joists projecting from a wall to create a porch or balcony floor without supports.

Carriage bolt A bolt with a slotless round head and a square shoulder below the head that embeds itself into the wood as the nut is tightened.

Caulk Tube-delivered plastic-and-silicon substance that cures quickly and is used to seal gaps in wood to prevent air or water leakage.

Cedar shingles Tapered 16- to 18-inch-long pieces of western cedar used for shims, siding, or roofing.

Check (in lumber) A defect in lumber caused by a separation lengthwise between the wood's growth rings.

Chords In triangular trusses, the wood members that form the two sides of the roof and the triangle's base.

Cleat A small board fastened to a surface to provide support for another board, or any board nailed onto another board to strengthen or support it.

Clinching The practice of driving an overlong nail through two boards and bending the protruding end over.

Code The rules set down by various regional code bodies that specify minimum building practices.

Collar tie A horizontal board installed rafter to rafter for extra stiffness.

Column A wood or metal vertical support member.

Common length in jack rafters The amount that jack rafters increase or decrease in length as they run between two angled rafters or an angled rafter and a top plate.

Common rafter Rafter in a gable-type roof that runs from the ridge to the double top plates.

Composite board Panel material similar to plywood but made up of reconstituted wood particles at its core and sometimes softwood veneer on its faces.

Core The middle veneer layer in plywood or the center section of material in a composite panel.

Corner boards One-by or 2-by boards nailed vertically to the corners of a building that serve as a stopping point for siding and as an architectural feature.

Cornice Also called roof overhang, the part of the roof that overhangs the wall.

Cricket A small gable-like structure installed on a roof to divert water, usually from a chimney.

Cripple studs Short studs that stand vertically between a header and top plate or between a bottom plate and the underside of a rough sill.

Crosscuts Cuts made width-wise, or across the grain of lumber.

Crown The natural bow along the edge of a joist, rafter, stair stringer, or other member. It should almost always be placed facing up.

Cup A distortion in wood across the grain caused by warpage.

Dead load The weight of the building components, including lumber, roofing, windows, doors, and flooring.

Deflection The bending of wood due to live and dead loads.

Diagonal bracing 1) Braces running from corner to corner used to stiffen walls and prevent racking. 2) Braces nailed off to cleats or stakes to support a standing wall.

Door sill The same as a threshold. A piece of lumber beveled along each edge and nailed to a floor to cover a floor joint or to mark a door passageway.

Dormer A shed- or doghouse-like structure that projects from a roof and can add space to an attic.

Double top plate The double tier of two-by lumber running horizontally on top of and nailed to wall studs.

Drip edge A metal piece bent to fit over the edge of roof sheathing, designed to shun rain.

Drywall Gypsum sandwiched between treated paper. Used as an interior covering material. Also called gypsum board or wallboard.

Eaves The part of a roof that projects beyond its supporting walls to create an overhang.

Elevation The same as height. When referred to in transit use, the height above or below a transit instrument.

End grain The end of a crosscut piece of wood.

Expansion bolt A bolt used to anchor lumber to masonry walls. The jacket of an expansion bolt expands to grip the side walls of a pilot hole due to wedge pressure at its base or the wedge force of a bolt screwed into it.

Facade The exterior front of a building.

Face-nailing Nailing perpendicularly through the surface of lumber.

Factory edge The edge finish put on wood and panels at the mill.

Fascia One-by or 2-by trim piece nailed onto the end grain or tail end of a rafter to form part of a cornice.

Fiberglass Spun glass fibers used in insulation and roof shingles.

Finishing nail A smooth nail with a tiny round head, normally set below the surface of finished wood with a countersink tool, or nail set.

Fire blocking Horizontal blocking installed between studs to defeat the upward progress of fire.

Flakeboard The same as particleboard.

Flashing Thin aluminum or copper strips or coil stock used to bridge any space between roof and framing, shingles and framing, or windows/doors and any part of the structure. Also, the metal strips used to protect corners and valleys in roof construction.

Floor plans Drawings that give a plan view (bird's-eye view) of the layout of each floor of a building.

Footing The base, usually poured concrete, on which a foundation wall is built. With a pressure-treated wood foundation, a gravel or soil footing may be used.

Framing anchor Metal straps, pockets, or supports used to reinforce or strengthen joints between wood framing members.

Frieze board Trim board nailed horizontally on a building wall directly beneath rafters to provide a nailing surface for soffits and cornice trim.

Frost line The maximum depth to which soil freezes in the winter. Frost lines change regionally.

Furring strips Narrow 1-by or 2-by wood strips used to create space—for example, between ceilings and ceiling joists or between insulated walls and masonry walls.

Gable end The triangular section at the ends of gable roofs.

Gable roof A triangular-shaped roof.

Gambrel roof A roof design common on barns and utility buildings that combines two gable roofs of differing slopes. Sometimes mistakenly called Dutch Colonial-style roof.

Gauge A measurement of wire thickness. The higher the gauge, the thinner the wire.

Girder A horizontal wood or steel member used to support some aspect of a framed structure. Also called a beam.

Girder pocket The let-in and seat created in a foundation wall in which a girder sits.

Glue-laminated lumber Stacked dimension lumber glued together to create a beam.

Grade 1) The identification class of lumber quality. 2)

Glossary

Ground level. The slope of the ground on a building site.

Ground-fault circuit interrupter (GFCI) A device that detects a ground fault or electrical line leakage and immediately shuts down power.

Gusset plates Metal or plywood plates used to hold the chords and webs of a truss together.

Gypsum board See "Drywall."

Hardwood Wood that comes from deciduous trees.

Header The built-up horizontal framing member that runs above rough openings to assume the loads that would have otherwise been carried by the studs that have been removed or omitted below to create the opening.

Heartwood The part of the wood between the pith and the sapwood.

Heel (rafter) When a rafter is in position at pitch, the end grain of a rafter closest to the rafter's underside.

Hip jack rafter A rafter that runs from a top plate to a hip rafter.

Hip rafter A rafter that runs at a 45 degree angle from the end of a ridge to a corner of a building.

Hip roof A roof that has a central ridge and that slopes in all four directions.

I-beam A beam, typically steel, with a vertical middle section and flat webs on the top and bottom.

Incline (roof) Same as pitch.

Jack rafters Short rafters that run between a rafter and a top plate or between two rafters.

Jack stud See "Trimmer stud."

Jamb The finished frame of a doorway.

Joist Framing lumber placed on edge horizontally, to which subfloors or ceilings are attached.

Joist hanger Bracket used to strengthen the connection between a joist and a piece of lumber into which it butts.

Kerf A shallow slot cut into a piece of lumber usually measured by the width of the saw blade.

Keyway A flat-bottomed notch or indentation created at the top of a footing to allow foundation walls to interlock.

Kiln-dried lumber Wood dried in a kiln, or a large oven, rather than by natural air currents.

Lag screw A large screw with a pointed tip and a hex head.

Lally column A steel pipe usually filled with concrete and used as a support column beneath girders and beams.

Ledger A horizontal board attached to a beam or other member and used as a shelf-like support for lumber that butts against the beam.

Level A hand tool for checking that any piece is perfectly horizontal or vertical. Also a term meaning horizontal.

Live load All the loads in a building not part of the structure—furniture, people, snow, wind.

Masonry wall A wall made of concrete, cinderblock, or brick.

Mastic A thick, pasty adhesive.

Miter box A hardwood open-topped square box with precut cut lines to guide angled or square saw cuts.

Moisture content (in wood) The amount of water contained in wood, expressed as a percentage of the dry weight of wood.

Mudsill Same as sill plate.

O.C. An abbreviation for "on center."

Oriented-strand board (OSB) Panel material made of wood strands purposely aligned for strength and bonded by phenolic resin.

Overhang The part of the tail end of a rafter that projects beyond the building line. Often it's enclosed by a soffit.

Particleboard Panel material made from wood chips and flakes held together by resin.

Partition wall A nonload-bearing wall built to divide up interior space.

Penny Abbreviation: d. Unit of measurement for nail length, such as a 10d nail, which is 3 inches long.

Pier (concrete) A round or square concrete base used to support columns, posts, girders, or joists.

Pilot hole A hole drilled before a screw is inserted to defeat splitting.

Pitch (roof) Loosely, the slope or angle of a roof; technically, the rise of a roof over its span.

Plates Horizontal two-by lumber at the top and bottom of a wall, or any horizontal lumber at the base of a wall.

Platform framing The framing method that builds walls, one story at a time, on top of platforms that are built on joists.

Plumb Vertically straight. A line 90 degrees to a level line.

Plywood A wood panel composed of cross-laminated veneer layers.

Prehung door A door that's already set in a jamb, with hinges (and sometimes a lockset) preinstalled, ready to be installed in a rough opening.

Pressure treatment A factory process of using pressure to force preservatives into wood.

Pump jack A working platform system that is raised and lowered along vertical 4x4s using a pumping action.

Quartersawn lumber Lumber milled from quartered logs, typically very stable, close-grained wood.

Rafter table The table of rafter lengths and cut angles found etched in the side of a framing square.

Rebar Short for "reinforcement bar." Metal bars laid in a grid used to reinforce concrete.

Resilient flooring Flooring that has memory and returns to its original shape after it is indented, usually made of vinyl and available in large sheets or smaller tiles.

R (resistance, in insulation) The measure of a substance's resistance to heat flow. An R-value is a number assigned to thermal insulation. The higher the number, the better the insulation.

Ridge The highest point of a roof.

Ridgeboard The horizontal board that defines the roof's highest point, or ridge.

Ridge cut The cut at the uphill end of a rafter, along the ridge plumb line, which allows the rafter's end grain to sit flush against the ridgeboard.

Rim joists Joists that define the outside edges of a platform. Joists that run perpendicular to floor joists and are end-nailed to joist end grains are known as header joists. Also called band joists.

Rip To cut wood in the same direction as the grain.

Rise In a roof, the vertical distance between the supporting wall's cap plate and the point where a line, drawn through the outside edge of the cap plate and parallel with the roof's slope, intersects the centerline of the ridgeboard.

Rough sill The horizontal framing member that defines the underside of a window's rough opening.

Run In a roof with a ridge, the horizontal distance between the edge of an outside wall's cap plate and the centerline of the ridgeboard.

Sapwood The living wood near the outside of a tree trunk that carries sap.

Scab A short piece of wood nailed on the face of two boards where they join to help position or strengthen them.

Scaffold A temporary working platform and the structure that supports it.

Scarf joint Where the end grain of two pieces of lumber meet in the same plane at a 45-degree angle.

Seat cut (rafter) The horizontal cut in a bird's mouth that fits on the top plate of a wall or horizontal framing member.

Shakes Same as cedar shingles, but rougher in texture because they are split rather than sawn.

Shear wall A wall, typically covered with carefully nailed plywood, that is designed to resist lateral force.

Sheathing Panel material, typically plywood, applied to the outside of a structure on which siding is installed.

Shed roof A roof that slopes in one direction only.

Shim A thin wedge of plastic or wood (typically cedar) used as blocking to level or plumb doors, windows, and framing lumber.

Siding Finish material applied to the outside of a building, either on top of the sheathing or directly nailed into studs and blocks.

Sill (window) The piece of wood at the bottom of a window frame, typically angled to shun water.

Sill anchor Threaded metal anchors set in concrete to which mudsills are attached with washers and nuts.

Sill plate The horizontal two-by lumber attached directly to the masonry foundation on which stand the building's walls. Same as sole plate and mudsill.

Slab-on-grade Monolithic concrete foundation that serves as both the building's first floor and the structure's perimeter footings.

Sliding T-bevel An adjustable pivoting straightedge that can be set at a number of different angles. Also sometimes called a bevel square.

Slope The rise of a roof over its run, expressed as the number of inches of rise per unit of run (usually 12 inches). For example: 6 in 12 means a roof rises 6 inches for every 12 inches of run.

Soffit The board that runs the length of a wall, spanning between the wall and the fascia on the underside of the rafters.

Sole plate Same as sill plate.

Span Distance between supports, such as the outside walls of a building or a structural wall and a beam.

Staging Same as scaffold.

Staple Hand or pneumatically driven U-shaped metal fastener used to hold shingles, roofing, and finished wood in place.

Story pole A piece of lumber (usually a 2x4) marked off in required dimensions to determine stair-height layouts and other elevations.

Stud Vertically standing two-by lumber that extends from the bottom plate to the top plate of a stud wall.

Subfloor Structurally rated plywood or oriented-strand-board decking installed on sleepers or joists.

Tail (rafter) The base, or downhill end, of a rafter.

Tail cut The plumb or square cut at the tail end of the rafter.

Theoretical rafter length The rafter length before it is shortened to accommodate ridgeboard thickness.

Timber Lumber pieces, larger than a nominal 4x4, typically used as columns or beams.

Toe-nailing Driving a nail at an angle into the face of a board so it penetrates another board beneath or above it.

Tongue and groove (T&G) Boards that have a groove on one edge and a tongue on the other so that other similar boards can fit into one another along their edges.

Top plate The horizontal two-by board nailed to the top of wall studs.

Total rise The ridge height of a roof measured from the top plate of the structure's wall.

Total run One half the building span.

Transit A telescope mounted on a swiveling plate that can view a perfectly level line 360 degrees once it has itself been leveled.

Trim One-by lumber used as siding corner boards or as finish materials around windows and doors, under eaves, or around cornices.

Trimmer joist A second joist added to reinforce a floor joist that defines a rough opening in floors.

Trimmer rafter A second rafter added to reinforce a rafter that defines a rough opening in roofs.

Trimmer stud Stud that runs from the bottom plate to the underside of a header. Also called jack stud.

Underlayment Highly stable, often water-resistant veneer-type panel material (a kind of plywood) installed on top of a subfloor but beneath resilient flooring or other finish floor material.

Unit rise Number of inches a common rafter will rise vertically for every 12 inches of run.

Unit run Unit of the total run, based on 12 inches for common rafters and 17 inches for hip rafters.

Valley jack rafter A rafter that extends from a valley rafter to a ridge.

Valley rafter A rafter that extends from a ridge to an intersecting corner of a building or to another rafter.

Veneer A thin piece or section of wood, typically a layer of plywood.

Waferboard Panel material made from wood wafers bonded with an exterior-grade resin.

Waler Horizontal lumber pieces used to span or stiffen walls.

Wallboard See "Drywall."

Warp Uneven shrinkage in wood causing bending or twisting.

Web (truss) The truss's inner members that tie together the chords.

Index

Index

Photo Credits

All photography by Steve Cory unless otherwise noted.
All illustrations by Ian Worpole unless otherwise noted.

page 1: Harperdrewart/Dreamstime **page 2:** Bobby Parks **page 9:** Lmphot/Dreamstime **page 10–11:** Pattie Steib/Dreamstime **page 12:** *upper right and lower left* Clemens Jellema; *lower right* Bobby Parks **page 13:** Bobby Parks **page 14:** Susan Law Cain/Dreamstime **page 15:** *upper right* American Deck and Patio; *middle left* Crystal Craig/Dreamstime; *middle right* Calyx22/Dreamstime; *lower right* Bobby Parks **page 16** *left* Harperdrewart/Dreamstime; *right* Christopher Nuzzaco/Dreamstime **page 17:** Susan Law Cain/Dreamstime **page 18:** Clemens Jellema **page 19:** *all* Bobby Parks **page 20:** Bobby Parks **page 21:** *both* Bobby Parks **page 22:** *upper right* Clemens Jellema; *bottom* Lmphot/Dreamstime **page 23:** *upper left and lower right* Clemens Jellema **page 24:** *left* Bobby Parks; *right* Melanie Baker/Dreamstime **page 25:** *bottom* Bobby Parks **page 26:** *both* Susan Law Cain/Dreamstime **page 27:** *right* Michael Shake/Dreamstime **page 28:** *upper left* Imagepointphoto/Dreamstime; *lower left* Clemens Jellema **page 29:** Clemens Jellema **page 31:** *left* Bobby Parks; *right* Lmphot/Dreamstime **page 32:** *both* Lmphot/Dreamstime **page 33:** Kim Katwijk **page 34:** *top* Gary Marsh; *bottom* Bobby Parks **page 35:** *top* Clemens Jellema; *bottom* Bobby Parks **page 36:** Clemens Jellema **page 37:** *top right* Bobby Parks; *bottom right* Pattie Steib/Dreamstime **page 38:** *top* Mark Hryciw/Dreamstime; *bottom* Clemens Jellema **page 39:** Bobby Parks **page 41:** *both* Bobby Parks **page 42:** Clemens Jellema **page 43:** *left* Bobby Parks; *bottom right* Clemens Jellema **page 44:** Lmphot/Dreamstime **page 45:** *left* Clemens Jellema; *right* Bobby Parks **page 53:** *bottom* Clemens Jellema **page 57:** CertainTeed **page 58:** CertainTeed **page 60:** *top right* Freeze Frame Studio; *bottom right* Bobby Parks **page 61:** *right* Bobby Parks **page 63:** bottom left Clemens Jellema **page 66:** John Parsekian/CH **page 67:** John Parsekian/CH **page 68:** John Parsekian/CH **page 69:** *top* John Parsekian/CH **page 70:** Alexandra Cory **page 71:** *bottom left and middle* John Parsekian/CH **page 72:** *top right* Clemens Jellema **page 77:** *bottom right* John Parsekian/CH **page 78:** *both* John Parsekian/CH **page 79:** *top left and right* John Parsekian/CH; *bottom* Alexandra Cory **page 86:** *bottom* John Parsekian/CH **page 87:** *bottom left and right* John Parsekian/CH **page 90:** *top right* John Parsekian/CH **page 124:** *top left* Kim Katwijk; **page 149:** *top right* Susan Leggett/Dreamstime **page 154:** *top left* Bobby Parks; *bottom left* Freeze Frame Studio **page 172:** *top right and bottom left* Bobby Parks

Builder Consultants

Jim Craig, Craig Sundecks and Porches
Stephens City, VA (540) 869-4333
www.craigsundecks.com

Clemens Jellema, Fine Decks, Inc.
Owings, MD (410) 286-9092
www.finedecks.com

Bobby Parks, Peachtree Decks
Alpharetta, GA (770) 667-2650
www,peachdecksandporches.com

George Drummond, Casa Decks
Virginia Beach, VA (757) 523-4505
www.casadecks.com

Cedar Works
Detroit, MI (248) 363-1113
http://cedarworks.net

Deckmasters Construction
South Elgin, IL (847) 429-9376
www.deckmastersconstruction.com

American Deck and Patio
(800) 592-3325
www.amdeck.com

Metric Equivalents

Length

1 inch	25.4mm
1 foot	0.3048m
1 yard	0.9144m
1 mile	1.61km

Area

1 square inch	645mm^2
1 square foot	0.0929m^2
1 square yard	0.8361m^2
1 acre	4046.86m^2
1 square mile	2.59km^2

Volume

1 cubic inch	16.3870cm^3
1 cubic foot	0.03m^3
1 cubic yard	0.77m^3

Common Lumber Equivalents
Sizes: Metric cross sections are so close to their U.S. sizes, as noted below, that for most purposes they may be considered equivalents.

Dimensional lumber	1 x 2	19 x 38mm
	1 x 4	19 x 89mm
	2 x 2	38 x 38mm
	2 x 4	38 x 89mm
	2 x 6	38 x 140mm
	2 x 8	38 x 184mm
	2 x 10	38 x 235mm
	2 x 12	38 x 286mm
Sheet sizes	4 x 8 ft.	1200 x 2400mm
	4 x 10 ft.	1200 x 3000mm
Sheet thicknesses	¼ in.	6mm
	⅜ in.	9mm
	½ in.	12mm
	¾ in.	19mm
Stud/joist spacing	16 in. o.c.	400mm o.c.
	24 in. o.c.	600mm o.c.

Capacity

1 fluid ounce	29.57mL
1 pint	473.18mL
1 quart	0.95L
1 gallon	3.79L

Weight

1 ounce	28.35g
1 pound	0.45kg

Temperature
Fahrenheit = Celsius x 1.8 + 32
Celsius = Fahrenheit - 32 x 5⁄9

Nail Size and Length

Penny Size	Nail Length
2d	1"
3d	1¼"
4d	1½"
5d	1¾"
6d	2"
7d	2¼"
8d	2½"
9d	2¾"
10d	3"
12d	3¼"
16d	3½"

Have a home improvement, decorating, or gardening project? Look for these and other fine Creative Homeowner books wherever books are sold.

The complete manual for plumbing projects. Over 775 color photos and illustrations. 304 pp.; 8^1/$_2$" × 10^7/$_8$"
BOOK #: CH278205

Complete DIY tile instruction. Over 550 color photos and illustrations. 224 pp.; 8^1/$_2$" × 10^7/$_8$"
BOOK #: CH277532

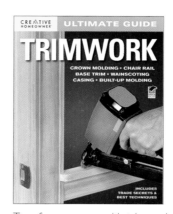

Transform a room with trimwork. Over 975 photos and illustrations. 288 pp.; 8^1/$_2$" × 10^7/$_8$"
BOOK #: CH277511

The ultimate home-improvement reference manual. Over 300 step-by-step projects. 608 pp.; 9" × 10^7/$_8$"
BOOK #: CH267870

Complete source book for molding trim. Over 1,000 color photos and illos. 256 pp.; 8^1/$_2$" × 10^7/$_8$"
BOOK #: CH279402

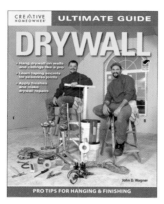

A complete guide, covering all aspects of drywall. Over 380 color photos. 176 pp.; 8^1/$_2$" × 10^7/$_8$"
BOOK #: CH278330

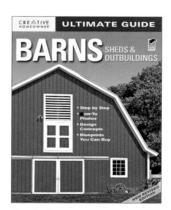

Plan, build, and finish a utility building. Over 975 color photos and illustrations. 288 pp.; 8^1/$_2$" × 10^7/$_8$"
BOOK #: CH277815

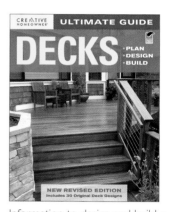

Information to design and build a deck or patio. Over 900 photos and illos. 368 pp.; 8^1/$_2$" × 10^7/$_8$"
BOOK #: CH277170

Inspiration for creating an attractive, up-to-date kitchen. Over 500 color photos. 224 pp.; 8^1/$_2$" × 10^7/$_8$"
BOOK #: CH279412

Great deck ideas from top designers. Over 450 color photos. 240 pp.; 8^1/$_2$" × 10^7/$_8$"
BOOK #: CH277382

The quick and easy way to grow fruit and vegetables. Over 300 color photos and illos. 224 pp.; 8^1/$_2$" × 10^7/$_8$"
BOOK #: CH274557

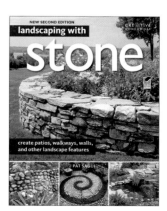

Ideas for incorporating stone into the landscape. Over 335 color photos. 224 pp.; 8^1/$_2$" × 10^7/$_8$"
BOOK #: CH274179